The Living Stress Free Bible

12/12/18

Kate

Hope this helps bring you more Peace, joy, and inspiration. Have a stress-free 2019! with many more to follow!.

Fondly, Marilyn

The Living Stress Free Bible

20 TECHNIQUES TO MAKE YOUR LIFE LESS STRESSFUL

Marilyn Sydlo Guadagnino

Marilyn Sydlo Guadagnino LCAT MT-BC
Living Stress Free, Inc.
Rochester, New York

ISBN-13: 978-0-578-40311-3

Dedicated to Louis J Guadagnino who opened my mind, my heart, and my awareness to new ways of perceiving my experience of the world and everything in it. You have been a catalyst for fulfillment in my life and your love carried me through all the hurdles along the way.

Thank you to my Meditation Masters who showed me the way to access true wisdom and universal knowledge, literally changing my life.

Much gratitude to the wonderful people I have had the privilege to work with as your therapist and counselor. Helping you with your struggles and your breakthroughs has taught me more than you can ever know. You are the basis for why I wrote this book. My life has been enriched by your willingness to include me in your journey to health and wellness and allowing me the honor of witnessing your transformations.

Thank you also to Benjamin Edwardsen for assisting me with his editing expertise.

Contents

Preface · ix

Introduction · xv

Chapter 1   The Third Door · 1

Chapter 2   Target Practice · 5

Chapter 3   The Bubble Machine · 9

Chapter 4   Your Secret Love Affair · 15

Chapter 5   Pet the Cat · 21

Chapter 6   Put Down the Magnifying Glass · 28

Chapter 7   Mindfulness: The Curiosity Cure · · · · · · · · · · · · · · · · · · 33

Chapter 8   The Allure of Escapism · 38

Chapter 9   Exhaustion · 44

Chapter 10   Velcro Past · 50

Chapter 11   Annihilate the Worrywart · 55

Chapter 12   The Age of Rage · 62

Chapter 13   Can You Truly Be Happy? · 68

Chapter 14   Getting Out of Your Own Way · 74

Chapter 15   Emotional Deliberation · 81

Chapter 16   The Best Meditation Technique You Can Do · · · · · · · · · · · · · 87

Chapter 17   Music Therapy, Mindfulness, and Healing · · · · · · · · · · · · · · 94

Chapter 18   Balance in All Things: The Yantra · 104

Chapter 19   Stress to Success in Six Months or Less · · · · · · · · · · · · · · · · 114

Chapter 20   Putting It All Together · 122

Appendix   Twenty-Six Additional Living Stress Free Practices · · · · · · · · 127

              About the Author · 135

              About Living Stress Free Inc · 137

Preface

The American author Henry David Thoreau wrote, "Do what you love. Know your own bone; gnaw at it, bury it, unearth it, and gnaw it still." I resonate with this quote because I love what I do. I am a mental health therapist. I have been able to teach people with varying degrees of debilitating stress, to feel better and do better since 1988. After thirty years, I still love my work, feel inspired, and look forward to seeing my clients every day.

I have contemplated why this is, why I love my work so much. Was it the fact I enjoy the role I have with people as a therapist and counselor due to the knowledge and support I have to give them? That was part of it, but not the main reason. I've wondered whether it was the fact that I've gotten better at my skills the longer I practice them, which feels fulfilling. That too, was not the real reason, although it is accurate. The real reason for my love of my work has nothing to do with me. It is all about what I learn from every person I meet with. It's not about me at all, it's about them. They are my teachers.

I don't do therapy with people; I have inspiring conversations with them. These conversations not only help clients gain insights and process their thoughts and feelings, they help me become a happier, healthier, more fulfilled person. This book is a compilation of that inspiration.

The "Queen of Jazz" Ella Fitzgerald once shared, "Don't give up trying to do what you really want to do. Where there's love and inspiration, I don't think you can go wrong."

The content of this book comes from those "ah-ha" moments during meaningful conversations with people suffering from too much stress. Through these discussions, unfolding the layers of thought, emotion, and discontent, amazing answers arose spontaneously. These insights are not from a psychology class in college, not from a trending therapy model, and not from a workshop I attended to get continuing education credits. The insights in this book came from inspiration and awareness, and the ability to tune into that awareness with openness and trust.

I have discovered when you have a meaningful conversation with another person, and you are completely in the moment with them, you are listening from the place of pure awareness, undisturbed by your mental agendas. From this place of pure awareness, inspiration and wisdom flow freely. Most of the time this wisdom is exactly what the person needs to hear to help their stressful situation. You, as the listener, really had nothing to do with that wisdom. It did not come from you. It came through you, much like seeing the pebbles at the bottom of a clear, still lake.

Alan Watts, a British philosopher, writer, and speaker, endlessly inspires me. He is quoted as stating, "This is the real secret of life — to be completely engaged with what you are doing in the here and now. And instead of calling it work, realize it is play."

I've learned to be the "clear still lake" when helping others from my own practice of meditation and yoga. I was very fortunate to learn genuine meditation practices from authentic meditation masters since 1992. For many people, knowledge of meditation and yoga came from a book, class, app, or Youtube video. This is limited knowledge, and often times inaccurate. I was able to meet enlightened masters, followed their directives, and practiced their techniques from several mainstream meditation paths for decades. The only way to gain sustained results from these helpful, ancient techniques is through consistently increasing knowledge and experiencing the practices. I have to say, the reason I love being a therapist and Living Stress Free Counselor is from my experience with meditation and yoga.

To briefly clarify, when discussing meditation in this book I am referring to the original practice of nondirective meditation, which is the practice of connecting with inner, core awareness, the silent space within, beyond the mind's thoughts and feelings. It is not contemplating a word, phrase, or image. In fact, no thought is intentionally engaged at all. It also has nothing to do with any religious faith. Nondirective meditation is an ancient practice that allows the meditator to experience the transitory nature of everything in existence and learn how to experience life through the lens of pure awareness. It is mindfulness to the max!

When the word yoga is discussed in this book, it refers to the philosophy of yoga. Most people are very familiar with yoga in terms of Hatha yoga, the physical expression of yoga. Yoga, however, has many forms, physical being only one of them. Yoga means union and balance. Yoga is the art of balance in all things. As the book unfolds, more will be discussed about these concepts.

Living Stress Free is not only the title, it refers to the stress reduction system and philosophy that all facets of Living Stress Free Inc promote. LSF is often used as an abbreviation throughout the book.

How will this book help you? Living Stress Free will make your life feel less stressful by changing the way you perceive your day to day existence. We all experience stress, and chronic stress results in a lack of fulfillment, dissatisfaction, disappointment, and discontent. More severe versions of accumulated stress interfere with functionality, causing excessive anger and rage, anxiety attacks, depression, and mental confusion. This book will help you overcome these challenges. It will also give you tools to share with loved ones who are struggling with stress overload. Let's face it; stress is an epidemic that is creating havoc for people physically, mentally, emotionally, and spiritually.

If you have serious mental health symptoms, this book alone may not be the answer for you. I would recommend using the book's suggestions in conjunction with more traditional mental health supports. However, if you are just stressed and not struggling with serious mental health symptoms, ask yourself are you best helped by medical model traditional mental health approaches, designed for more serious symptoms, or would you benefit from a practical, nuts and bolts self-help approach? Living Stress Free is practical self-improvement, with simple wisdom, designed to not only decrease and manage stress but to help prevent it from forming in the first place.

I am indebted to the meditation teachers who helped me progress in my ability to navigate this complicated, stressful world. When learning a life-transforming practice such as meditation, a student must work with someone who has forged ahead and has the knowledge and experience to impart to others. I am forever grateful to my spiritual teachers and meditation masters who have taken that journey to its fruition and continue to help me with my personal development and self-improvement.

I also must acknowledge what my husband, best friend, and business partner has done to make this book possible. It was his wisdom, insights, and encouragement that helped me become a better therapist, a better meditator, and progress on my own spiritual path. He is the creator of all the foundational practices and philosophy of the Living Stress Free Program. Lou Guadagnino has a wealth of knowledge and experience that continues to unfold through Living Stress Free Inc.

I gratefully acknowledge my clinical experience as a music therapist. The fusion of art and science that has produced music therapy and the creative arts is such a valuable offering to the healthcare field. I am fortunate to be able to approach mental health treatment from this angle, offering out-of-the-box perspectives and innovative strategies to enhance traditional medical model treatment.

This book is perfect for anyone who is sick of feeling stressed and is looking for a new perspective, an open-minded approach, with practical solutions towards personal development. It is not based on medical model research or clinical trials. Having worked for a university hospital for decades, I am knowledgeable and supportive of evidence-based practices, but I have also seen how the cookie-cutter approach of one size fits all treatment is not always effective. I acknowledge the work the mental health field is doing, but it is not for everyone. Living Stress Free can help those with whom traditional methods have not helped or those who have no experience in therapy or counseling and want to "cut to the chase" and find relief from stress fast.

One of my favorite role models for success is Steve Jobs. He is quoted as saying, "You've got to find what you love. And that is as true for your work as it is for your lovers. Your work is going to fill a large part of your life, and the only way to be truly satisfied is to do what you believe is great work. And the only way to do great work is to love what you do."

Given the crazy world, we are living in, there is no better time than now to learn new tools to live stress-free. I truly love my work: learning how to live stress-free and helping others move toward this intention. I have found that the most effective helpers in the world present as a combination of clinician, healer, and innovator. That is what I offer you in this book: the tools for personal growth and healing. Some of the clients I have provided counseling for have shared how they never thought about these ideas before, were never taught these strategies, and yet the perspectives outlined in this book helped them more than years of therapy. These ideas, strategies, and perspectives are here for you. This book was written for YOU. It will guide you through this journey to living stress-free.

Introduction

iving Stress Free. Whenever I say these three words to anyone I always get a reaction. Some of my favorite cynics say, "Yeah right, like that could ever happen." My Type A Personality friends say, "I like to feel stressed; it motivates me to get things done." There are also the cautious curious ones who say, "Oh, that would be nice, is that even possible?" This last group is actually the majority. *both me*

Whether you are a cynic, a Type A go-getter, or an inquisitive stressed person, you will change your perspective on how to navigate your stressful life after reading this book. Living Stress Free is applicable to all, with no exceptions. All I ask is you keep an open mind and entertain the concepts without filtering them through the "I already know this" screen that often exists in people's minds. My favorite zen author Shunryu Suzuki wrote: "In beginner's mind there are many possibilities, in the expert's mind there are few." Take in the words of this book with fresh eyes instead of automatically comparing it to something you already know.

What is "Living Stress Free?" I'll start by telling you what it's not. Here are four common myths:

Myth I: Living stress-free means you will never experience stress again.
That is impossible. Stressful circumstances occur every day and you have no control over that. What you do have control over is how you perceive those stressful situations.

Myth II: Living stress-free means you are sitting on a beach doing nothing for the rest of your life.
On the contrary, the goal of Living Stress Free is to have a fulfilling life balanced with work, play, enjoyable relationships, and opportunities to learn and grow, with health, happiness, and success in all areas.

Myth III: Living stress-free interferes with achievement and motivation.
Believe it or not, the less stress you experience the more efficient, productive, and creative you will be. Stress can lead to feeling overwhelmed which is a motivation killer. Less IS more and "no pain, no gain" is a philosophy that is helpful with marketing exercise videos, but not in all areas of life.

Myth IV: Living stress-free is impossible.
This is untrue; don't let anyone tell you otherwise. The secret is in changing how you perceive the inevitable stress that enters your life. Once you change your relationship with whatever is bothering you, you change your experience of it.

Living stress-free is the purpose and end result of this book. I will teach you how to be free from the effects of stress by giving you tools to experience stressful situations in a different way. I will also offer strategies to release the stress that has accumulated within your body and mind that has a tendency to cause excessive anxiety, agitation, disempowerment, or rage in response to circumstances that do not merit such a strong reaction. Lastly, the techniques presented in this book will help prevent stress from settling into your body and mind to begin with. This will help you succeed in all areas of life, with ease.

Before I go any further, it would be helpful to define stress from the perspective of Living Stress Free. Stress refers to the inevitable byproduct of any event, situation, belief, emotion, mood, or behavior that interferes with our natural needs. To put it more simply, anything that knocks off your balance produces stress. This is why vacations are stressful, even though they are fun. This is why you have stomach issues after eating a holiday feast.

The frustration you feel from not finishing your to-do list causes stress. Too much attention to the news and strong feelings about a particular politician causes stress. Insomnia, oversleeping, excessive exercise, inactivity, self-consciousness, loneliness, too much pleasure, not enough pleasure - all of these disturb your balance and cause stress. This is a much wider definition than most people are used to. Stress goes way beyond just feeling overwhelmed.

Even the idea of good stress — eustress — qualifies as stress from this perspective. If stress is helping a person get a task completed or provides the extra boost to push through the struggle, it is having an effect on the body and mind that is disturbing natural balance. This is not to say you should never push yourself to accomplish amazing things or forge ahead even though it is causing blood pressure to increase and a rapid heartbeat. The goal is to be aware of the effects of stress and to make choices accordingly, given your own necessities, value system, and path in life.

To understand stress we have to take a moment to review the mechanism of a stress reaction. Our ancestors lived in a different world. Primitive societies had life-threatening dangers such as wild animals that attacked them. They experienced acute stress which activated the fight-or-flight reaction to defend themselves. The brain produced stress hormones during fight-or-flight that caused the body to tense and heartbeat to increase; cortisol and adrenaline rushed to muscles to provide the ability to react for self-preservation and survival. When the danger was over the body returned to normal. In modern society, there are two strikes against us. Our version of wild animals attacking are the stock market crashing, being fired from a job, car accidents, and abusive relationships, just to name a few examples. In addition, we experience a chronic version of stress when feeling trapped in a situation there is no way out of. The brain continues to produce these stress hormones the same way it did for our ancestors, taking a toll on our mind and body.

Stress hormones are harmful to the body when they are overproduced. They were meant for short-term activation. Sadly, this is not the case for many people. We live in a stressed society that seems to value the qualities in life that tend to produce more stress such as competitiveness, over-achievement, and producing more with fewer resources. Every time stress hormones are traveling through the body, they have a negative effect on the body. If it's occasionally, the body can handle it, but if it's frequently, it will take its toll on our health and wellness.

Stress manifests in three different ways. The first way is the obvious one. There is an immediate stressor, such as someone cutting in front of you in a car, producing a reaction. You hit the brake automatically, the body tenses, and you usually gasp, yell, or even curse. Your body temperature rises, heartbeat quickens, and breathing becomes rapid and shallow. This is adrenaline and cortisol fueling your reaction. After the stressful event is over, you quickly return to your normal, balanced state. This is what LSF refers to as transient stress. It comes and goes quickly.

LSF calls the second form of stress residual stress. With residual stress, it takes longer for the body and mind to return to its balanced state. For example, a death of someone you care about will linger in your thoughts and feelings, causing crying spells, angry thoughts, and other cognitive and emotional reactions. Your body will experience fatigue, the immune system lowers its ability to fight cold viruses and infections, and your sleep may be affected. The grief reaction stays with you for a period of time, and you slowly return to your balanced, normal state. This residual stress works its way out on its own, as times passes.

The third way stress manifests, according to Living Stress Free, is accumulated stress. This is the most dangerous. Basically, accumulated stress is the old stress that never got released. Difficult situations occurred in the past that never got processed. Much like food needs to be digested and metabolized, thoughts and feelings also need to be metabolized. This occurs through processing: contemplating the event, acknowledging the feelings and talking to trusted supports about it, and sometimes journaling or expressing it in other creative ways in order to release it. These difficult situations from the past affected you in some way that resulted in the events getting stuck inside the mind-body instead of being processed. This "old stress" sits in the tissues of the body and can cause secondary problems such as chronic pain, chronic gastrointestinal issues, and depression or migraines, just to name a few. Trauma victims experience the effects of accumulated stress quite frequently. This is the most difficult type of stress to release and most trauma survivors just put a Band-Aid on it by taking medication, overindulging in alcohol or drugs, or becoming workaholics. As you learn the tools outlined in this book, you will have the means to release accumulated stress once and for all.

Here's an important question I'd like you to contemplate. When you feel very stressed, why do you tend to gravitate toward behaviors that won't help you in the long run, behaviors that are actually counterproductive to helping your body and mind? For example, you are very upset about an argument with your boyfriend, and the first reaction is to eat an entire container of ice cream. Or maybe the results of your blood work were not what you expected, and your first desire is to go have a cigarette. Binge watching Netflix all day when you have work to be done, excessive drinking, or chatting with negative angry friends, are just a few other examples. You know that your self-improvement books, inspirational videos, church friends, and helpful coping skill handouts would all help but you don't want to go in that direction. Why? Because like attracts like. Stress seeks out experiences that are on the same level as itself. Worse yet, if you're like most people, you feel bad about yourself for indulging in unhealthy behaviors and this self-criticism only worsens the stress. It is an endless loop.

This same principle affects problem-solving. If you are stressed and that same stressed mind is trying to problem solve, guess what? The solution is filtered through a stressed perspective which means it may not be the best solution. Albert Einstein once said, "We cannot solve our problems with the same level of thinking that created them." If our thinking mind is reinforcing our stress, we cannot think our way out of it. It is on the same level, the same playing field. The best way to effectively problem solve is to calm down, regroup, and return to your default state of being centered, grounded, and aware. Once you have returned to this state, you won't have to make a choice because you will naturally know what to do. This is what you will learn in this book.

Living stress-free is not a remote possibility or silly idea. It is most definitely possible. You live stress-free by changing your relationship with stress, which is anything that interferes with your balance. To approach stress in this way goes beyond the common stress management techniques currently on the market. This book will change your attitude and perception of your life. That is what all of us have control over - how we perceive each situation we experience. It is not the stressful circumstances that cause our worry, frustration, and panic; it is our thoughts about the stressful circumstances that unravel us. As you weave your way through these pages, you will be given the tools to change your perspective to improve your experience of this life you have been given. This will lead to increased contentment, satisfaction, happiness, and fulfillment. You will not only experience life in a more positive way, you will enjoy your own company once again.

This is what Living Stress Free will do for you:

1. Teach you how to manage the transient stress that arises each day so your reaction to the stress changes — Decrease stress in the present.
2. Teach you how to release the residual and accumulated stress that is still within you, affecting your mind and body — Dissolve stress from the past.
3. Teach you how to avoid stress from disturbing your inner peace throughout your life — Prevent stress in the future.

In these twenty chapters, I will teach you specific strategies and techniques to seriously lower your stress and increase happiness, health, and fulfillment in all areas of life. This is how you succeed with ease. At the end of each chapter, review the "LSF Takeaway" that includes a brief synopsis of the main theme of that chapter and a suggestion for how to practice the specific strategy discussed. As a special bonus, be sure to explore the Appendix which offers one practice per week for twenty-six weeks. This is a great way to reinforce the skills taught in this book in a practical, structured way. In six months or less, you will watch your life transform from stressed every day to relaxed, alert, productive, happy, inspired, and content. I invite you to also explore livingstressfree.org, the foundational resource for information on how to lower your stress and live a happier, healthier life.

CHAPTER 1
The Third Door

As a child of the 70's, I grew up watching game shows almost every day. One significant memory I have from a particular game show, Let's Make a Deal, was when Monty Hall asked the contestants to choose which door had the prize — Door #1, Door #2, or Door #3. If the contestant chose correctly, they would walk away with a brand new car, an amazing vacation, brand new furniture or other extravagant prizes.

Over time, the premise of this simple game became a probability theory based on assumptions and mathematical equivalencies called the "Monty Hall Problem." This dilemma challenges one to analyze the best strategy to win the game, whether it is to stay with the initial choice, or whether to explore percentages, probabilities and battle the ever-present "what ifs" stirring in the brain.

As a young girl, I was not concerned with any of these mental conundrums. Sir Isaac Newton once wrote, "Truth is ever to be found in simplicity, and not in the multiplicity and confusion of things." Being a lifelong fan of simplicity, I was just pleased to watch the contestant win the car!

As I got older, I began to look at those three doors in a new way. It is easy to perceive life through the lens of duality. We can always see two doors. For any situation, no matter what the circumstance, most of us can see two options; two possibilities for dealing with the issue. For many people, this boils down to the "good" decision or the "bad" decision, the positive or the negative, right or wrong, black or white, hot or cold, day or night, and so on.

We live in a world of opposites and make most decisions based on polarity. What if there was a third option, a third door? What would happen if we took the time to explore another way of looking at the situation? I have worked as a mental health therapist for thirty years. Through my experiences helping so many different people with problems, symptoms, and challenges, I have discovered one of the most helpful strategies a person can do for another is to show them the third door. There is always another way to perceive a situation outside of the obvious choices. All it takes is going beyond the natural tendency of the mind to polarize the issue and explore other angles and ways of thinking and feeling.

Why do we polarize situations so much? I've contemplated this question many times and what I've discovered is not all people get stuck in duality. If the community a person dwells in is very focused on good, bad, right, wrong, dogma, and societal dictates, the person living in that community will have a more dualistic, polarized perception of all their circumstances. In contrast, communities in which people follow natural rhythms and function more from their experience and less from their ideas and beliefs, seem to be able to entertain a myriad of perceptions and possibilities. Society obviously has a need for laws and guidelines for people to follow, but this can certainly be taken too far. When rules interfere with an individual's ability to explore issues independently and think for themselves, inadvertently fostering "sheep mentality," the tendency towards polarization increases.

Another cause for dualistic thinking is the "us and them" perspective. Whenever we perceive a separation from others due to ideology, political viewpoints, religious affiliation, cultural differences, economic status, race, sexual orientation, gender, age, etc., there is polarity. Perceiving this separation externally only reinforces this same tendency internally, with thoughts and feelings. This feeling of separation sows the seeds of anxiety, worry, and fear.

The philosopher, speaker, and writer, J. Krishnamurti wrote, "When you call yourself an Indian or a Muslim or a Christian or a European, or anything else, you are being violent. Do you see why it is violent? Because you are separating yourself from the rest of mankind. When you separate yourself by belief, by nationality, by tradition, it breeds violence. So a man who is seeking to understand violence does not belong to any country, to any religion, to any political party or partial system; he is concerned with the total understanding of mankind."

When faced with a challenging issue, if only two solutions arise, this polarized perception will create anxiety that will force the stressed person to choose a side and make a quick decision to relieve the anxiety. The problem is this decision was made from a stressful state of mind. It may not be the best solution. Worse yet, the decision may not resolve the issue and it will return, causing an endless loop of stress repeating itself.

I have a Quartz Crystal in my office. I love to gaze at it and notice the different sides the form of the rock displays. It is the perfect metaphor for seeing different sides to any situation. Sometimes I hand it to a client as we explore different options and ways of looking at their dilemma. We loosen the rigid dualistic perception, and allow for "not knowing." Not knowing is not easy for most people. Knowing is seen as a sign of intelligence, capability, and success. Being "in the know" is an honored trait. However, if you study the ancient wisdom from the Yogic, Taoist, and Buddhist traditions, to not know is what is most valued. The Upanishads, ancient Vedic texts, state: "He who knows, knows not. He who knows not, knows." There is intelligence in not knowing.

Another problem with only seeing two sides of an issue is ambivalence. When you cannot make a decision and feel stuck between two opposites, stress increases. Ambivalence always creates stress. There is fear in identifying with one side or the other because you might make the wrong decision. One of the best antidotes for ambivalence is to allow for a third option and then sit with it, allowing it to percolate. The third door will loosen up the polarized perception and ease the mind enough for the light to come in. Chapter Fifteen offers an innovative technique called Emotional Deliberation to take this dilemma of ambivalence to the next level. If you're struggling with this issue right now, you may want to jump ahead to that chapter for more direction to find your way.

LSF Takeaway #1

Perceiving more than two sides of any situation is extremely helpful for exploring the "bigger picture." A more expanded perspective and increased awareness can help make more informed choices and better decisions. Whenever you are uncertain and caught between two ways of looking at something, always explore the third option. If you have difficulty, ask a friend, colleague, or other trusted person in your life for assistance. There is always the third door and you will be amazed at how knowing this will relieve your stress.

Third Door Worksheet

Dilemma:

_____

_____

_____

First Explanation:

_____

_____

_____

Second Explanation:

_____

_____

_____

Third Explanation:

_____

_____

_____

CHAPTER 2

Target Practice

One of the first things I realized when I started working with people to help improve their ability to function was how often they identified with their stress and were unable to see beyond it. They forgot about the healthy part of them, whether they decided it was covered up or completely gone. They were so familiar with struggling they could not perceive life without it.

Whatever a person identifies with, they become. For example, if you see yourself as a nervous person, you will reinforce that habitual tendency to become attached to nervousness. This cultivates and solidifies it. The same is true for low self-esteem, neurotic tendencies, and addiction, to name just a few examples. You become so familiar with these identifications you eventually cannot see anything else. It becomes whom you think you are.

The other side is true as well. If you identify with the healthy parts of you, you will shift your experience of who you are. The more you perceive yourself as relaxed, content, happy, accomplished, confident, and loved, the more you will experience this state of mind. The well-known practice of reciting or writing down positive affirmations is based on this truism.

If all of this is true, why doesn't everyone just do this? Why don't we approach each day with complete conviction that all is well within and without? Because for many people, it's too unfamiliar. Feeling stress, focusing on stress, and experiencing stressful situations is a very common way of living for many people. People get so accustomed to feeling stressed, they become stress itself.

I work with a client named Sally. Sally was sharing one day how she perceives the different parts of herself and what she would like to change regarding her relationships, physical health, and recreation. When I asked her about her mental health and what she would like to change about herself, she replied, "I would still have depression, anger, and negative thoughts and feelings because that is who I am. Without those, I would not be me." This is a great example of a person's identification with what's wrong becoming so familiar it cannot be taken away even if given the opportunity.

Since stress reactions dwell in the mind, it behooves us to contemplate the question: What does perfect mental health feel like? While this is an important question to ask ourselves, our society will not support this contemplation, from my observation. The media and many people we interact with on a daily basis will focus on what's wrong, not what's right. We will engage in conversations each day based on describing what is stressing us. This "water cooler talk" can be quite counterproductive to reducing stress.

What is the experience of perfect mental health? What does the stress-free mind feel like? If you want to get there you have to know what you're shooting for. It's our essential target practice. However, this is a difficult question for many people to answer because it's so unfamiliar. The qualities you identify with will set the stage for your future, so it is an essential question to answer. Healthy change requires a change in perception.

Perfect mental health without stress interference is possible. I have had the good fortune of watching people improve and gravitate towards perfect mental health. I've experienced my own journey towards the goal of having a stress-free mind. You can achieve this too!

One of the most enjoyable activities I had the pleasure to experience in high school gym class was archery. The calm, precise skill required in archery can teach you a lot about life. The skill involves holding the bow correctly, pulling back the arrow purposely and releasing at the proper moment. However, it all starts with looking at your target and knowing where the arrow is going. In the same way, knowing how you want your thoughts and feelings to arise is helpful when cultivating the mental health you are looking for. When you know your target you can shoot your arrow accordingly.

Here is my personal description and affirmation of what perfect mental health and stress-free living feel like:

- I feel contentment, cheerfulness, and love as my normal state.
- Emotions and feelings arise and I allow them to be in my awareness without reacting. I respond as needed or just accept the feeling until it passes.
- My thoughts are clear, effective, and inspired.
- I am spontaneous, quick-witted, and have a good sense of humor.
- I can problem solve with ease. I know the correct response at any given time, which may include no response.
- When I indulge in thoughts about memories from the past or plans for the future I do not get carried away and can stop at any time.
- I can let things go.
- I live in the present moment with alert curiosity.
- My mind does not control me.

Now it's your turn. Take some time to envision what your perfect mental health experience would be like. Be as specific as possible. What would make you thrive, feel empowered, and enjoy your own company? How would you experience your feelings and your thoughts? What would living stress-free feel like? This is your personal target practice! Begin to set the stage for your renewed state of mind. Write it down. When you see it in front of you it will solidify and begin to take root in your life. Read your description each day to become familiar with it. You cannot reach the goal of living stress-free if you cannot envision it. You cannot create healthy change if you are not aware of what you seek.

Novelist Sir Terry Pratchett wrote, "If you do not know where you come from, then you don't know where you are, and if you don't know where you are, then you don't know where you're going. And if you don't know where you're going, you're probably going wrong."

LSF Takeaway #2

Whatever you identify with, you become. What you think about yourself right now sets the stage for how you will feel in the future. Imagine if you had perfect mental health and you no longer have stress. What would that be like? How would thinking and feeling change for you? You cannot achieve that which you cannot envision. Use "I" statements and describe what living stress-free feels like.

This is how I will think and feel if I was living stress-free:

_____

_____

_____

_____

_____

_____

_____

_____

_____

_____

_____

_____

_____

_____

_____

_____

_____

_____

_____

_____

CHAPTER 3
The Bubble Machine

"All experiences are preceded by mind, having mind as their master, created by mind" - Buddha. This chapter is dedicated to understanding the mind, the origin of thought, and the process of thinking. In Yogic philosophy, from the teachings of the Bhagavad Gita, the mind is likened to a sixth sense. Long ago, entire civilizations perceived the mind as no different from the eyes, ears, nose, tongue, and skin: a vehicle for sense perception. This is an interesting way of looking at the mind that seems to have great relevance in modern day society as well. The mind's job is to create thought. If the mind is seen as a sense, it drastically changes its function and the power it appears to have over our lives.

What is thought? A thought is basically a vibration of energy. First, there is silence. Out of silence a spark of energy is ignited. The energy vibration forms into a thought. This thought occurring in the mind is always based on memory — 100% of the time. The thought may or may not lead to a feeling. The feeling may or may not lead to an action. However, the basic progression is thought — feeling — behavior. Awareness of this alone can be transforming because it provides a roadmap to trace the origin of action. But there's more!

There is a distinct difference between thought and thinking. A thought is generated by the mind from past impressions and will pass on its own. Thoughts behave much like cars going by on a road, or boats on the water.

Your mind is in control of this process and you cannot stop it in any sustainable way. When you choose to engage with a thought, either consciously or unconsciously, you begin the process of thinking. You do have control of thinking. Here's where your mind can be your best friend or your worst enemy, and everything in between.

You cannot control thought but you can control thinking. Have you ever noticed you think about certain thoughts and hold onto particular thoughts frequently? Maybe this is due to a desire for something you want. Or maybe it's due to a dislike for something, an aversion, an injustice, a negative experience. This thinking becomes a habitual pattern and before you know it, it's automatic. You feel like you cannot stop thinking. This is a perfect recipe for stress in the form of worry, resentment, regret, hopelessness, or feeling overwhelmed, just to name a few examples. It definitely doesn't lend itself to contentment and relaxation.

I work with a client we will call William. William often tells me in sessions how he has bad luck in relationships and cannot stay in a relationship longer than a month. He comes to therapy to try and figure out if it's him or them. Through our sessions, it became clear he is somewhat obsessed with the idea of being in a good relationship that leads to marriage and children. He wants this more than anything. The fact it has not happened has led him to blame himself and think negatively about who he is. He often says self-critical statements spontaneously in the sessions. He has stated he cannot stop thinking about this. We have tried many techniques to balance his perspective and look at other areas of his life for fulfillment but he cannot get this desire out of his head. He is highly stressed and his thinking mind is habituated to this dilemma. He is not alone in this affliction.

I invite you now to set aside any preconceived notions about your mind and explore this metaphor: your mind is a bubble machine. Imagine your mind is a machine that is designed to create bubbles. You've probably seen these bubble machines at a child's birthday party or maybe on stage for a scene in a play or a concert. The bubble machine keeps on churning out bubbles endlessly, much like your mind creates endless thoughts. The bubble machine uses bubble liquid to create bubbles and your mind uses past experiences to create thoughts. Whatever happened to you in the past affects your perception of what the mind creates. It is all filtered through the impressions from your past. All thought is based on memory. Thoughts about the future are anticipations based on past experiences. You even perceive the present through the filter of the past by comparing everything you experience now to something similar from your past. The bubble liquid is your past and the mind creates bubbles from it. You don't experience life: you experience your thoughts about life.

This metaphor is extremely helpful for learning what to do with your thoughts. If you see your thoughts as bubbles it is easy to imagine them floating by. It also makes it easier to avoid grasping the thought because you cannot catch a bubble — it will pop. This can help decrease the habitual pattern of overthinking.

Sigmund Freud once said, "Where does a thought go when it's forgotten?" This is beautiful to contemplate. The thought is gone and has lost its reality. This is not a sad fact, it is a helpful tendency. Why try and remember endless thoughts? Let them go like bubbles and the ones you need to remember you can write down or deposit into your "note to self" mental database and trust it will return when needed.

Thinking is necessary for problem-solving, goal setting, and deductive reasoning, but it is not necessary 70% of the time. We waste enormous amounts of energy thinking too much to indulge our fantasies, addictions, obsessions, neuroses, and convictions. Many thoughts are not real, not factual, and not true. The sooner we understand this the better we will feel and the lower our stress will be. "It's just a thought" will prove to be the best response in many situations.

Perceiving thoughts as bubbles helps you notice the space between the bubbles, referring to the space between your thoughts. That space brings you to the default state of silence in the mind, where the thought was created. This silence is pure awareness, ever present. It is also the place where creativity and inspiration arises.

The renowned Taoist teacher Lao Tzu has said, "Silence is a source of great strength." When we are fully present and aware with a silent mind, dwelling in the space between the bubbles, we are infinitely effective and capable, no matter what the situation.

Music is a wonderful example of how to perceive thought and thinking. As a particular song is played, if you become preoccupied with the introduction you would not hear what comes next in the song. Instead, if you listen as the song progresses, hearing the melody, harmony, and rhythm, noticing how each new phrase begins, you will not cling to anything that was already played. You will just enjoy the song, being in the moment, as it unfolds.

Similarly, becoming preoccupied with a thought and choosing to think about it, not paying attention to whatever task you are doing, will prevent you from being alert, effective and fully present. Thoughts are like a musical soundtrack playing in your mind. Let the song play without clinging to the song. It's just background music while you go about your day.

It is easy to mistake reality for thought because you have been conditioned to do this. Thoughts are just vibrations of energy. If a random car drives by while you sit on your porch, does the car have any importance in your life? If a thought arises while you sit on your porch, do you have to give it importance? It's just a vibration of energy that's fueled by your past experiences and impressions. That's all it is.

You have been conditioned to give credence to thoughts, as if they are a message from God, to take as fact. If the thought is based on the past, how can it be a reality? The past is remembered differently depending on whose perception you are listening to. Did you ever participate in a holiday gathering where family members are sharing an event or situation from the past? Inevitably, you will hear several different versions of the same situation depending on who recounts it. We filter our past experiences through our own mental screen and perceive our memories differently. Why would you cling to the past and treat it like it has absolute reality? The past is over and life goes on, things change, existence progresses, our reality is ever new. Thoughts will take you away from reality. Reality exists in the here and now.

If thoughts are not reality or fact, should you ever listen to thought? This is a great question. The answer exists in knowing the difference between habitual thoughts based on past impressions and inspired thought. When you hang out in the spaces between thoughts, when you sit in silence, you open the door for inspired thought. An inspired thought is new, creative, fresh. It comes from the silence of meditation, yoga, tai chi, the moment before you fall asleep or before you wake up. It is present whenever you are completely in the here and now, not engaging your thoughts. An inspired thought is the seed of creativity and is not of the mind. It comes from awareness. It gives you a jolt of creative energy that feels like a connection with something greater. It is a beautiful thing. The less you engage the endless bubbles the more you leave space open for inspired thought.

I have noticed in my interactions with both clients and personal relationships in my life that people are addicted to thinking. If a person is not thinking they feel anxious like a security blanket was taken away. It is the human condition to get lost in the storyline and narrative of thinking and create a false reality to increase comfort and familiarity, only to find that life takes over and messes with our vision. The more detailed the storyline the more problematic it can be.

Changing this tendency to be addicted to thinking will take some time. As the famous medieval French phrase states, "Rome wasn't built in a day." Awareness is the first step. Here are seven main ground rules for increasing awareness and changing your relationship with your thoughts:

1. Trying to control thoughts is impossible. Controlling thinking is very possible, and a helpful practice.
2. Trying to clear your mind is impossible to sustain.
3. Thoughts are simple — they arise and pass. Thinking is complicated.
4. The more a person thinks, the more complicated they perceive their life.
5. The more excessively you think, the more you are missing the reality of the present moment.
6. The details of thinking are ultimately not as important as the reality of the present moment.
7. See your thoughts as vibrational patterns instead of getting lost in the thinking process of details and storyline.

Practice the bubble machine technique when you find yourself ruminating, overthinking, craving, desiring, raging, impatient, intolerant, worrying, or just too serious about something causing you to miss out on the experience of the present moment. Awareness alone is your greatest asset and can cultivate change purely through the awareness process.

LSF Takeaway #3

Changing your relationship with your mind is the key to reducing your stress and feeling more fulfillment, contentment, and stability. Knowing how thought is formed, the difference between thought and thinking, and what to do with your thoughts is the key to reducing and preventing stress.

Take a blank piece of paper and set a timer for two minutes. Write down every thought you have during the two-minute time period. After you're finished, ponder this question: Did you notice you were thinking about your thoughts or were you just observing a succession of random thoughts? This is the first step to noticing your mind bubbles. Identifying with the part of you observing your thoughts increases your ability to be fully present and aware. As you go through your day, start to become aware of the moments you are able to let a thought go and the times when you hold onto a thought and become distracted with thinking.

Record Your Thoughts for Two Minutes

_____

_____

_____

_____

_____

_____

_____

_____

_____

_____

_____

CHAPTER 4
Your Secret Love Affair

Undoubtedly, you have experienced the feeling of being in love. It's that intense fixation and fascination with a person, place, or thing that overcomes you and can interfere with your day to day tasks and activities. You become mesmerized by the idea of the object of your affection and everything else becomes less important, if not an annoyance. Everyday life pales in comparison to the attention you hold towards the idea and feeling of being in love. Unfortunately, this exciting feeling often prevents you from functioning optimally and effectively. Mario Teguh, an Indonesian businessman and motivational speaker, is quoted as saying, "Never make a decision when you are upset, sad, jealous, or in love."

What most of us do not realize is the greatest love affair in anyone's life by far is the love affair we have with our own mind. We are fascinated by our thoughts and feelings. It is how we define ourselves. It forms our identity and our sense of self. We enjoy our thoughts, we entertain ourselves with thinking, and we indulge our feelings. Unequivocally, our relationship with our mind is the most intimate relationship we have.

This truism is important to be aware of because the love affair with the mind can be quite problematic. For example, a person can be in love with their thoughts about a person but have no ability in reality to have a relationship with them. Are they really in love with the person or their thoughts about the person? The same is true for any infatuation or attachment. The attachment is to the thoughts of the person, place, or thing, not the reality of the person, place, or thing.

All of life is this way. The side effect of paying too much attention to thoughts and getting lost in feelings is that life is no longer experienced — our thoughts about life are experienced. Thoughts become more important than the reality of the moment.

A great example of this is the harp player at the wedding. You attend a wedding and during dinner, there is a lovely lady playing the harp in the corner of the restaurant. She performs a beautiful repertoire of different musical selections for two hours nonstop. Unfortunately, the conversation is loud in the room and she can barely be heard. The next day when telling your friend about the wedding you state, "It was so nice, they had harp music during dinner." Did you actually hear the music? Do you know any songs that were played? What was the musician's name? These questions cannot be answered because the reality of the harp music was lost, only the idea that there was harp music was held onto. It was an incomplete experience.

This happens all the time, every day, in small ways as well as significant ones. You go to a summer festival because the idea of spending a Saturday at an outdoor event sounds good to you. Once there, you regret having gone. It's crowded, too hot, there is nowhere to park, the food is expensive, and you are disinterested in what is being offered there. The idea was a world away from the reality. What's the result of this? Disappointment and frustration — you could have spent the day differently. These negative feelings may have been avoided by looking more deeply at the reality of the actual experience of the event and making the decision to go based on this, not just the idea. Learning to live by reality instead of thoughts and ideas alone is the secret to contentment and fulfillment.

I have gone down that road before with watching the Fourth of July fireworks. I love fireworks. They are always beautiful to watch and bring the viewer directly into a state of mindfulness — being fully present in the moment. I have not seen fireworks in years because of dealing with where to sit comfortably so the view is good, coping with how late it ends on a work night, and navigating the traffic after the show is over. Last year, my husband

and I decided to go see the fireworks. It started with the idea of watching fireworks. We then explored where the best venue would be given the parking issues, seating concerns, and other details. We turned the idea into the reality of what the experience would actually be like. After the display, we were stuck in the parking lot for forty-five minutes, I got home late and had less sleep for work the next morning, but there were no negative feelings or bad reactions to the experience. It was completely fulfilling. This was because my expectations were based on reality and not my ideas.

Sometimes major life decisions are made based on ideas alone which can lead to detrimental results. Peter, for example, might like the idea of being a college professor, but the reality is in conflict with his ideas. He finds it is difficult to teach the way he prefers due to the dictates of the educational institution who hired him. To change careers would be like starting all over again. Take the example of Cynthia, who might like the idea of getting married but ends up feeling unhappy because she chose her spouse, not because of the reality of who the person is, but the idea that it would be nice to be married or a desire for children. Over time the marriage inevitably has problems. These situations and countless others can have lifelong consequences because decisions were made on the level of thought and idea alone and not from the level of awareness and reality of the present circumstances.

We create a strong relationship with our ideas, which are the combination of thoughts and feelings. We identify with them, we own them, and nurture them. They fill the empty spaces when we are not engaged in an activity and distract us when we are in the midst of activity. Why is this relationship so strong? Because many people feel like this is who they are.

We can become identified with thoughts as "my thoughts" or feelings as "my feelings" which then form "my ideas." We then use this identification to define who we are and to feel special. Ever notice when you're depressed it's "your depression" and you see it as special as if other people don't really know what it's like. This is normal; it's the human condition. However, if one moment you're sad, another moment you're angry, and the next moment you're laughing, who are you? You're definitely not your feelings and emotions because they come and go. You don't come and go. You never left!

The same is true for thought. Thoughts come and go like bubbles, as discussed in the previous chapter. We are not defined by our thoughts because they are transitory. When we think about a thought over and over, contemplating it, stirring up feelings about it, ideas are formed that begin to comfort us and give us a solid identity. We hold onto those ideas as beliefs and that becomes our reality. But how can any of this be our reality if it's based on a thought that is a passing vibration of energy? It is not reality, it's just a thought. It is not fact, it is not the truth. Reality is based on our experience of life. Our experience shows us fact and truth.

Back to the love affair you may be having with your mind. As most people who have been in love have learned, the fascination and attention on the object of your affection interferes with and disrupts your life. Fascination and attention on your mind equally interferes and disrupts your life. That's because fascination and attention are the same.

What can be done about this disruption? Cultivate awareness. Only through shifting your focus to the awareness of the actual situation can you see things as they are. Instead of one-pointed focus and concentration on your love affair, replace it with awareness of how it really is. Explore all sides and see beyond the superficial; open the "third door," as discussed in Chapter One. True awareness exists on many levels, not just the level of the mind. Practice awareness of thoughts, awareness of feelings, awareness of your physical body and its reactions, awareness of your breathing, awareness of your environment. This leads to a true experience of reality, through the perception of awareness.

Much like other love affairs, in time the intensity transforms one of two ways. Either the fascination dies down and you lose interest, or the fixation softens to a healthy, loving attention, grounded in awareness. That is the goal of how to deal with the mind. Be aware of thoughts and feelings passing, think when needed, and make decisions based on reality, not on ideas alone: there's what you think about life, and then there's life. The experience of life is the reality. Staying centered in reality is the best method for living life with fulfillment, contentment, and satisfaction. Living from our ideas about reality often leads to discontentment and a feeling as if something is missing or incomplete.

LSF Takeaway #4

Learning how to make decisions based on the reality of the situation instead of your ideas about it will improve your ability to live stress-free. Experiencing the present moment as often as possible is the best way to stay centered, grounded, and effective.

For one week, start to become more aware of when you are fascinated by your mind, distracted from the here and now. Examples include when you lose track of time, miss your exit while driving, or forget whether you took care of the laundry. Begin to identify what you were thinking about and write the themes in your journal. This will show you what is increasing your stress, disturbing your natural balance.

Significant Thinking-Themes Resulting in Distraction:
Monday

_____

_____

Tuesday

_____

_____

Wednesday

_____

_____

Thursday

_____

_____

Friday

_____

_____

Saturday

_____

_____

Sunday

_____

_____

CHAPTER 5

Pet the Cat

The Polish composer and pianist Frederic Chopin wrote, "I wish I could throw off the thoughts which poison my happiness, but I take a kind of pleasure in indulging them." Chopin was not alone. This tendency is part of the human condition.

This chapter will explore three tendencies of the mind that are part of the human condition: grasping, resisting, and ignoring. Your thoughts and thinking processes travel these roads. All three roads of the mind create stress; all three tendencies are inevitable; all three can be eradicated through the practice of observation and awareness.

Ever notice how your attention wants to gravitate to certain thoughts? Human beings tend to be creatures of habit and the mind is the source of that redundancy. Since you have such an intimate relationship with your mind, you have a tendency to hang out with it and follow it wherever it goes. Where you put your attention is what you honor and cherish.

Take Joe, for example. He is very good at making money and organizes his life in the most efficient way possible for making money. Joe's attention to money is what he honors and cherishes. He has an attachment to money; he grasps his thoughts about making money and plans his life around increasing his revenue. A second example is Melissa. Melissa just had her first child and is a new mother. Her attention is on her newborn baby. Melissa will nurture her attachment to her child because this helps her take care of her baby the best way possible to be a loving, caring mother.

Grasping, otherwise known as attachment, is one of the roads our thinking mind travels on and is often directed toward something helpful in life. Grasping can also be the road our thoughts ride on when it comes to addiction to a substance, desire for an audition to go well, or clinging to the hope that a loved one will heal quickly from a disease. Attachment to something we want is a natural, human tendency.

Grasping is not a quality to judge — it is a natural tendency of the mind. If you let go of the destination on the grasping and attachment road, you will see it's the same road regardless of the destination or the situation. All human beings have attachment, grasping, desiring, wanting, and clinging as a process in their mind. This can be a stress producing process because you can never have everything you want and you can never hold onto that which you have forever. Everything is transitory.

The Sufi mystic poet Rumi wrote: "If you want something, release the wish, and let it light on its desire, completely free of the personal."

There is another road the thinking mind travels on. When you are hanging out with your thoughts and they are focusing on what you don't want, you are riding the road of resistance and aversion. How often does your mind dwell on dislike of a particular politician, the dread of a mandatory meeting, desperation to not feel physical pain, or hatred for a circumstance that resulted in the loss of someone you loved? Where you put your attention is what you honor and cherish. You are inadvertently nurturing and reinforcing these negative thoughts and feelings the more you resist.

This is how people get stuck in a long-term chronic state of frustration, irritability, discontentment, and suffering. This is how guilt, jealousy, envy, feelings of unworthiness, and despair become inflated. This is the process of riding the car of resistance and aversion on the road of the mind.

I work with a client I will refer to as Jennifer. Jennifer suffers from chronic pain due to fibromyalgia. Whenever we meet, she tells me how terrible the pain is and how she wishes it would just go away. She keeps hoping for a new medication to help the pain subside. She is fixated on her resistance and aversion. Jennifer will only find relief from suffering if she drops the resistance and aversion to the pain.

Why do we do this to ourselves? Why do we nourish and magnify the very stress we want to get rid of? Because of the "love affair" we have with our mind and a lack of awareness. Our resistance and aversion turn into a solid idea that helps form our sense of identity — whom we think we are. In the case of Jennifer, she sees herself as someone in constant pain, struggling every day. It is whom she thinks she is.

How often does someone define themselves as cynical, critical or "a problem?" This comes from their habitual process of honoring their thoughts of resistance and aversion in the mind. There is so much they do not like that is happening in their life. People with this negative self-perception, I have noticed, are quite prevalent in our society. Clients have shared with me that even on Internet dating sites, when someone is describing his or her personality on his or her profile, one of the positive attributes listed is sarcasm, which is the art of shifting attention to the negative. Is sarcasm positive? Aversion and resistance is a road well-traveled.

The tendencies of grasping and resisting can both be problematic. They can interfere with your perception of reality and often prevent awareness, balance, and presence to lead your life. When caught in the habitual patterns of attachment (grasping) and aversion (resisting), you may miss out on other aspects of life. Whenever your experience of life is incomplete and out of balance, you will be left with dissatisfaction; a feeling like something is missing. This can lead to many forms of stress such as anxiety, depression, rage, panic attacks, phobias, addictions, insomnia, and regret.

There is one more tendency of the mind that interferes with reality. It is called ignoring. This tendency is subtle and not always seen as being a problem. While you are busy honoring and engaging the patterns of grasping and resisting, you are ignoring everything else. Picture yourself traveling the roads of attachment and aversion in your imaginary car of the mind, engaging the storylines and narratives of what you want and don't want, with blinders up on the sides of the car. Ignoring your environment, physical sensations, thoughts, feelings, people, and things disallow a complete experience of the moment. You miss out on life. Ignoring leads to many forms of stress as well. This is because that which you ignore is still there, whether you like it or not.

What is the antidote for honoring the three tendencies of the mind? Stress that is created through grasping, resisting, or ignoring can be released through the practice of awareness. Awareness is the ability to observe what is occurring in your mind as it is occurring. It doesn't mean anything needs to be changed. It means the answer is in the awareness that it is happening. Awareness can change habitual patterns just through the process of observing and getting out of your own way.

There is a part of you that is always present. It never comes and goes. It is permanent and never changes. This part of you has nothing to do with the three stressful tendencies of grasping, resisting, and ignoring. It is awareness: core awareness. It is the part of you that knows what you dreamt last night. It is the part of you that watches your thoughts. Awareness is always fully present. When time stops as you watch a meteor streak through the sky, you feel awareness. When you take the first bite of an amazingly delicious dessert and there is no thought, only the experience of the treat, that's awareness. You can access awareness anytime, anywhere. Specific ways to practice accessing your core awareness will be presented later in this book.

In terms of controlling the three stress producing tendencies of your mind, the first step is to begin to be aware of which road your thoughts are traveling on. Do you tend to have attachment thoughts, grasping for things you want? Do you tend to have aversion thoughts, resisting things you don't want? Or, do you tend to just ignore certain thoughts? It's interesting to see what your own personal tendencies are. All of us do all three, but most people have a tendency to stay on one road more than another.

The next step is acknowledgment. Whether the thoughts you are observing are based on grasping or resisting, it does not change the fact they exist and are stress producing. The best strategy is to honor these thoughts and release them. This is what I call "pet the cat". If you had a cat looking for attention, rubbing on you, nudging you, what is the best thing to do? Pet the cat! Put her on your lap, give her a little attention and she will happily jump off and be on her way. That's what you can do with thoughts and thinking processes. Acknowledge the thoughts are there, honor them, but then release them and let go. Just like a leaf floating on a stream, the thoughts keep moving along if we get out of the way. Even if the thought is difficult and painful, acknowledge it, honor it, and release it. Painful thoughts tend to stay with us because we try to get rid of them or we over-indulge them looking for answers. Neither will work; the thoughts will only strengthen. Trying to ignore any thought will not work either because it still exists. Pet the cat. With this knowledge, you can live in a state of awareness in the midst of whatever your mind wants to do.

It is important to remember the goal is not to stop the mind from thinking or stop yourself from grasping, resisting, and ignoring. The goal is to be aware of the tendencies of the mind and how this affects your thoughts, feelings, and actions. Using the cat analogy, the goal is not to get rid of the cat. The goal is to be aware of the cat's needs, honor those needs, and let her be. She will feel acknowledged but will not bother you. In the same way, acknowledge your thoughts and let them go. This will open up awareness to the greater experience of living in the present moment. This will reduce stress and increase feelings of contentment and fulfillment.

LSF Takeaway #5

The three tendencies of the mind that are a stress producing part of the human condition are grasping, resisting, and ignoring. Your thoughts and thinking processes travel these roads. Being aware of these tendencies and acknowledging your thoughts and feelings openly and honestly lead to an ability to let these stressors go.

To learn about the tendencies of your mind and which roads these patterns travel on, for one week, keep a tally of how many times you notice the following:

G — Grasping and experiencing attachment to specific thoughts and feelings of what you want.

R — Resisting and experiencing aversion to specific thoughts and feelings of what you don't want.

I — Ignoring and not acknowledging specific thoughts and feelings that are in your mind.

Place a "G" "R" or "I" each time you notice these tendencies on that day.

Monday _____

_____

Tuesday _____

_____

Wednesday _____

_____

Thursday _____

_____

Friday _____

_____

Saturday _____

_____

Sunday _____

_____

Did you notice you tend to engage in grasping more often? Resisting more often? Or do you tend to ignore the issues in your life that are causing you stress? This is not a judgment; it is an observation.

Now that you've started noticing these tendencies, as you go about your days and weeks, mentally label your thoughts as "grasping/attachment" or "resisting/aversion" instead of focusing on the details of what you are grasping or resisting. It's a tendency of the mind, not something to become fascinated by. Acknowledge this tendency and move on. Becoming more aware of the types of thoughts you are having will naturally decrease the tendency to ignore. In this way, the stress producing tendencies of the mind will not be able to affect you in the same way they did in the past. You will gain more control and progress towards your goal of living stress-free.

CHAPTER 6
Put Down the Magnifying Glass

We don't experience life; we experience our thoughts about life. The mind is always creating thoughts that are based on our past impressions. The mind is just memory —it's a purely mechanical process. These thoughts the mind creates seem real and form the basis for our ideas, beliefs, and convictions. We identify with these opinions as factual and correct. This is how most people go through life.

Through working as a therapist and my experience as a meditator, I can honestly say living life through the filter of thinking alone, and cultivating constant opinions and ideas, leads to stress in one form or another. It is easy to get fascinated with thinking and lose track of reality. It's the storyline that is created. Consequently, the ability to "pet the cat" and release the storyline becomes very difficult, if not impossible, at times.

As an example, let's examine Stephanie, who is a very busy person. Stephanie has about fifteen things on her to-do list, including several errands and even some deadlines that must be completed before her children come home from school at 3:30 pm. Her situation is extremely overwhelming. She is caught up in her storyline throughout the day. Her thoughts tell her: "how will I get through this ... I have so much to do ... why didn't I finish some of these errands over the weekend ... what if I don't get this done, my boss will be very frustrated with me ... Oh no, I forgot to contact my sister to see how her medical procedure went ... I wish the weather would warm up a little ... I need to go to the gym." This is storyline and storyline creates stress.

The goal is to notice thoughts arising and passing. When you begin thinking about your thoughts too much, maintain awareness that you are thinking, but continue to stay fully present and do the next task that needs to be done. Obviously, this is not always easy. Thinking turns into your own personal commentary about the thoughts you are thinking, much like the sports announcer chattering about the golf pro teeing up for his next swing. This commentary turns into an interesting storyline that you may have difficulty letting go of. This storyline has the potential to morph into obsessions, rumination, endless mental chatter, and constant second-guessing. You hold your imaginary magnifying glass to the storyline and become focused on it. The trick is to put down the magnifying glass!

Why is dropping the storyline so difficult? It is familiar and provides a sense of security. It is common for people to fear the unknown. Thoughts are from the past so they are known. That which is known provides a sense of hope, a feeling that things can get better. How often do you notice people who are very stressed have a wish that things return to how they were: "if only we can live the way we did in the past, everything would be ok." The truth is there were just as many problems back then as there are now, yet people still feel secure with the idea of returning to that which is known.

In my work with people who suffer from trauma, I have observed a tendency for the person to return to dangerous situations that are similar to the experience that produced the trauma because it is familiar. Trauma survivors are not the only ones who follow this pattern. Our past secures our existence. It reinforces our beliefs and the feeling that we are justified and right about what we do. If we exclusively listened to our mind all of the time we would live completely in the past, which is not healthy or realistic.

When you become fascinated by your thoughts and the storyline you create, a conflict between what you think and what you experience in reality occurs. This conflict leads to comparing, judging, and feeling dissatisfied. For example, if you go to a new restaurant and order the chicken soup, when you taste the soup you will automatically compare it to the other chicken soup experiences you have had in your life. You will then decide that the soup is "pretty good, but it was better at that restaurant I went to in Cleveland."

Although this is a small example, the truth is you probably do this with significant circumstances in life all the time. How often do you decide in your mind how your vacation is going to go before you even arrive? You plan a special date night with your spouse and get disappointed that it didn't unfold the way you hoped. If you stayed in the present, without expectations, the experience would most likely be a pleasant one.

I struggled with this tendency for years. I am a planner, and I always enjoy thinking about future projects, days off, long-term goals, and my bucket list. It is somewhat of an escape from "the now" but it also gives me direction for where I'd like to be. I come from a family that *really* celebrated birthdays. My mother always says that a person's birthday is the most important day of the year because they were born on that day. After growing up this way, and reaching adulthood, I had disappointing birthdays for years due to my own mind. I decided how I wanted it to be and created a storyline of expectation. I didn't realize other people were not raised with such celebration of birth. For two decades I did this and never felt completely satisfied. After I learned meditation and gained more wisdom about how the mind operates, I realized what I was doing to myself, and no longer experienced frustrating birthdays. The conflict between my thoughts and reality was resolved.

The most dangerous example of fascination with the past is related to addictions. The conflict between the past — including thought, feeling and behavior — and the present becomes such a struggle it can lead to dire consequences and an inability to function. The mind is remembering the addictive behavior and defaults back to it when the experience of the present is too stressful, too difficult, or too unpredictable. The tendency is to return to the "safe zone" and indulge in the familiar. That is why the best strategy for any addiction is mindfulness: learning how to stay fully present and cultivate awareness.

A perfect quote to describe this tendency of the mind is by the philosopher Alan Watts: "A person who thinks all the time has nothing to think about except thoughts. So he loses touch with reality, and lives in a world of illusion."

What can you do if it's difficult to put down the magnifying glass that keeps you focused on your storyline and thinking processes? Add, don't subtract. Do not try and stop these thoughts, rumination, or preoccupations. That will never work. You cannot stop the mind from having thoughts, especially habitual thoughts. Add awareness of your experience of the present moment including the feeling of breathing, the sensations of your physical body, the sounds in your environment, and sensory input.

If you had half a glass of grape juice with an overly intense taste that you could not drink or dump out, what could you do? Add water to the glass. The grape juice would not be gone, but it would be diluted, appear lighter in color, and taste less intense. Then it would be easier to drink. Do the same with your mind. When you are over focused on your thoughts, add the feeling of your body, the sounds in the room you are in, and the awareness of your exhalation. This will "dilute" the storyline of your mind.

In summary, be aware of paying too much attention to your thinking mind. When thinking turns into commentary and storyline, it will interfere with your experience of the present moment. Stop focusing exclusively on your thoughts. It will drain your energy and make you less effective. Put down the magnifying glass. Pay attention to everything in the here and now and just do the next thing. Before you know it, you will be living your life with more happiness and calmness, but also increased efficiency. Interacting with your environment as you perform your actions is often more important than interacting with your thoughts as you complete your tasks.

LSF Takeaway #6

Thoughts are generated by the mind, which is a database of past impressions. The mind is created by memory. The more involved we become with our thinking processes, the more we are at risk of missing the present moment. When we miss the present moment, we lose concentration, don't listen as well, and have difficulty retaining information.

Practice the following suggestion to change the habitual pattern of becoming lost in your storyline: Every time you begin a task or initiate an action, pretend it is the first time you are performing this action. Have the curiosity of a child and the openness to allow for fresh awareness while you complete your task. Over time, the mind will stay fully present with the moment as it unfolds, instead of already deciding how it will complete itself.

CHAPTER 7

Mindfulness: The Curiosity Cure

As we begin this next chapter, you are probably noticing "awareness" is mentioned in almost every chapter as an antidote to the worried, stressed mind. The Merriam-Webster Dictionary gives the definition of *aware* as, "having or showing realization, perception or knowledge." In other words, being aware means you know something. The awareness I am referring to is on a broader scale. If you limit awareness to just having some knowledge, it stays at the thought level; thoughts are based on the past. Following its mechanical pattern, your mind will compare your present experience of knowledge with memories of your impressions from the past. How can this change your habitual pattern of perceiving things? It just reinforces the same impressions you have always had.

Awareness, as it is used in this book, refers to mindfulness: the experience of the present moment as it is, using all the senses with alert curiosity, to perceive exactly what is occurring, not the *idea* of what is occurring filtered through the untrustworthy mind. It is ever fresh, ever new. Mindfulness is not an activity or skill; it is our very nature. Watch a newborn baby. Since his or her cognitive abilities have not been developed yet, the baby lives in a state of mindfulness. All of us started out this way, but our thinking mind became stronger and more developed, covering up the ability to stay in "the now" with alert curiosity. Treating each moment as fresh and new brings a sense of childlike joy and openness back to our experience of life.

There are several techniques that can help you achieve the ability to live in the moment with open awareness. The first technique is seeing each moment as different, not the same as in the past. If you listen to anyone who is disgruntled, irritated, or disheartened, you will always hear the person state something like this: "See, this is just like what happened before ... it figures ... why do I even bother ... " This type of thinking is completely disempowering and usually leads to anger, depression, and chronic negativity.

The truth is every moment is brand new. The present moment is always moving forward, it is never stagnant, and the future is unpredictable. What has not yet happened is still an untouched treasure that hasn't been opened. It has the potential to unfold in several different ways. If a person moves into the present with preconceived notions that it will be just like before, the future has then been skewed in a certain direction that weighs heavier for that result to occur. This is because the perception of the person set the stage. This is where the term "self-fulfilling prophesy" stems from. A person expects a certain result and that is what actually occurs. It is also this tendency that feeds an addiction, enhances an obsession, and cultivates depression. All of these mental states and others similar to these lead to misery.

You can experience right now the newness of every moment. Notice your breathing pattern as you are reading this. Notice as the air goes into your nose and the air leaves your nose. That was the last time you will ever take that particular breath at that particular moment. It was also the first time that breath was ever taken! You can do this by walking. Each step you take is the last time you will ever take that step in that way, at that moment. Imagine going through your day this way? What a new perspective of existence it would bring. The more you can experience the newness of each interaction, each task, each meeting, each meal, and each night's sleep, the more you will perceive each moment as different, not like before. This is an inspired way to live.

Another technique that is related to the newness of each moment is curiosity. This means complete curiosity, not just having a curious intellect. Mindful curiosity is being aware of your body and your senses. If you walk through a park and you are thinking the entire time, you have lost the experience of the park. However, if you walk through a park and notice what you see, what you hear, what you smell, and how the air feels, you are keeping open alert awareness — curiosity. One of the greatest poets from the New Thought Movement, Walt Whitman, wrote: "Be curious, not judgmental."

Beware of "curiosity killers." For example, if you drive to work the same route you take every day and you start noticing what is different on this drive than yesterday's drive, you are practicing curiosity. You notice the weather is different, traffic patterns have slightly changed, and different people are walking by at the intersection. If your mind starts comparing this experience to yesterday's, making judgments on why the traffic is so slow compared to usual, or reminding you that you may be late for work, you've lost the moment. Your mind became a "curiosity killer."

Curiosity, in terms of mindfulness, does not mean being curious about your ideas or agendas. It means experiencing what is: noticing the "is-ness" of life. One could call it acceptance, but it is more accurate to call it *allowing*. Acceptance sometimes signifies defeat or surrender. Allowing has no emotional reaction attached to it. For example, we allow the fact that food cools off when it sits on the table for a while. This is not something we must accept. The more you live with the attitude of allowing, the more you will naturally drop judgment.

Mindfulness teachers often state that mindfulness is nonjudgmental awareness and suggest this as a practice. There is no need to practice being nonjudgmental. If you go about your day allowing circumstances to occur, you will naturally drop seeing things as good or bad, and you will see things are as they are. It is a freeing experience. If you are serious about lowering your stress and decreasing worry, frustration, or negativity, *allowing* is a state of mind that will help tremendously.

It is important to acknowledge that people have difficulty with the unpredictability of life. Being open to the unknown factors of the future can cause anxiety, nervousness, and fear for some. If this resonates with you, look at this pattern more deeply. What aspect of "not knowing" causes worry? In most cases, the answer is a strong attachment to the mind and the thoughts created by past experiences. The past represents safety for many people.

It provides a sense of security and identity. If someone's personal history included factors that contributed to having very little to count on, it is understandable the pattern would exist to count on past memories. Expecting certain results to happen makes some people feel relieved. However, it does not lead to a feeling of calmness and fulfillment because life really is unpredictable. Life moves forward and holding onto the past is ultimately futile. The easiest way to slowly forge a path out of this tendency is through curiosity and seeing the newness of life as it occurs.

The novelist and poet Anne Bronte has a beautiful quote that exemplifies awareness itself: "And then, the unspeakable purity and freshness of the air! There was just enough heat to enhance the value of the breeze, and just enough wind to keep the whole sea in motion, to make the waves come bounding to the shore, foaming and sparkling, as if wild with glee."

LSF Takeaway #7

Awareness is mindfulness. It is the experience of the present moment, as it unfolds, without the thinking mind altering the moment with ideas, beliefs, or judgments.

For the next week, create a ritual at the end of each day to identify anything you noticed for the first time throughout your day. You can mentally take note or write down in your journal what you observed. Maybe it was the construction cones on the side of the road, maybe the way the sun streamed through the willow trees by the creek, maybe it was the color of your coworker's eyes, or maybe it was the music playing in the grocery store. The more you can notice and be aware of your experiences each day, the less you will be lost in your thoughts. The less you are lost in your thoughts, the less stress will accumulate.

"I never noticed this before ..."

_____
_____
_____
_____
_____
_____
_____
_____
_____
_____
_____
_____
_____
_____
_____
_____

CHAPTER 8

The Allure of Escapism

I remember when I was a young girl hearing the famous 1970's commercial that touted "Calgon, take me away," referring to a powdered water softener. The commercial featured a beautiful woman relaxing in her bathtub, taking a break from her household duties. It represented calmness, serenity, self-care, and happiness, and everyone wanted to experience what she was enjoying. That phrase stayed with me as the quintessential image that represented getting away from it all: escapism.

Escapism was popular then and it is safe to say escapism is even more popular now. People work hard. There is a lot of stress in our world. It is perfectly natural to want to get away from all the stress. I have had clients who shared with me their "short-term disability fantasies," in which they secretly hope they fall victim to a minor accident so they can be excused from work and other responsibilities for a few months. To be honest, I have contemplated that same fantasy at difficult times in my life as well. Nevertheless, we do not need to get hurt to have an excuse to take a break from life. That is why the first suggestion you will likely receive from family, friends, or professionals when you are feeling particularly stressed, is to distract yourself from it. This is the allure of escapism.

A friend recently sent me a wonderful cartoon featuring a drawing of three booths at a Spiritual Fair. One booth offered past life readings, another offered fortune telling for the future, and the one in the middle advertised "Present Moment Anyone?" As you might have guessed, the lines for the past life readings as well as for the fortune telling were very long, and there was nobody in the Present Moment line. This is not a surprise. Most people do not want to focus on the present when they can escape into the past or the future. In addition, all the thoughts the mind is creating are about the past and the future, so it feels comfortable to indulge this tendency.

Here's the problem with distraction — it is temporary. It is also inefficient. We must metabolize thoughts, feelings, and experiences just like we metabolize food. If we don't, they stay inside the mind and body just like undigested food. This can lead to accumulated stress that turns into negative states of mind, unexplained anxiety, panic attacks, or even physical illness depending on the amount of accumulated stress that is built up inside. The best way to prevent this from occurring is to fully experience the present moment by staying in it. Allow the thoughts, feelings, and actions that are in the present moment to flow naturally. Distraction and escapism prevent this process from happening.

As discussed in Chapter Five, the mind has three tendencies that lead to experiencing stress reactions: grasping, resisting, and ignoring. These tendencies are "red flags" of escapism. If you watch your mental tendencies when life is particularly challenging, you will notice your thoughts will gravitate to one of those three. You may get fascinated with your attachments. People who have addiction issues, for example, will nurture and honor their addiction more when they are stressed because it is distracting them from what is really wrong in their life. Others indulge in aversion and focus on how much they dislike certain people and blame them for all the problems in life. The truth is, this is escapism and a distraction from the real issues in the person's life. The mental tendency to ignore is the most obvious version of escapism. You put the blinders on and don't look in that direction. Beware of these red flags because they block the ability to digest the reality of the present moment, as it is.

If most people recommend distraction as a coping strategy to life and it is only a temporary solution, what can be done as a permanent solution to the stress reactions life presents? The answer is surprisingly simple: being fully aware of thoughts, feelings, and actions, allowing them to naturally unfold with each situation that happens as the day progresses — that is the key to lowering your stress. If you feel anger, allow yourself to feel angry. By blocking it, anger gets trapped inside. If you are grieving, allow the grief to be honored. If you are incredibly happy, express it! Do the same with your thoughts. Allow the thoughts to arise into your awareness but also allow them to leave. The only reason the thoughts will stay is if you choose to hold onto them. Even if the thought is disturbing you must remember it is just a thought, it isn't a fact. It can't hurt you. A thought is just a vibration of energy having its moment. Think of it like a firefly intermittently lighting up as you walk through the woods at dusk. Our thoughts are like fireflies.

Inevitably you may be wondering, "What if I get sad or angry at work? I can't express that in front of everyone. It will interfere with my job." This is a reality and the answer depends on the intensity of your emotions. If your feelings are on a softer level, you can let yourself feel in the midst of your work. If you needed to, you could take a few minutes to yourself to surrender to the emotion, compose yourself, and go back to the task at hand. However, if the feelings are too intense, self-care is paramount. You may need a temporary escape or distraction to help you finish your responsibilities. The important point is to allow the expression of emotions when you are somewhere appropriate to do that. Do not just bury the situation and forget about it without processing it. There may be times you need to take a day off and just allow the inner storm to flow. That is what mental health days are all about.

Another way to combat escapism is to see the different sides of the stressor: changing your perception of the situation. I remember years ago when traveling on the Garden State Parkway with my family, my father driving, witnessing a car speeding like mad past us in the other lane, cutting off another driver, tearing down the highway. My parents, feeling stressed, commented judgmental remarks about the driver, as most people who have driven on busy highways can relate to. I started sharing with my parents different scenarios for why the person was speeding: maybe he is rushing to get to the hospital, maybe he is very late for work and is afraid he might get fired, maybe he needs to get to a special family event such as a wedding and is in danger of missing it? My father would eventually start smiling and the stress reaction of the moment dissolved. In the same way, you can stay fully present and entertain alternate solutions and explanations for absolutely everything if you allow yourself to do this.

This method can be used with your own emotions as well. There is a benefit as well as a challenge to all the emotions. Anger is seen as bad, but anger also energizes. Depression and sadness are dreaded, but when you experience them you catch up on your rest. Happiness is seen as golden, but it can lead to getting lost in elation and losing awareness of the present moment due to becoming overly excited. Mistakes can then occur. If good and bad are taken off the table, you can see the different sides of all thoughts, feelings, and experiences. Judging, comparing, and deciding there is a hierarchy of emotional states and thoughts can be detrimental to managing and preventing worry and stress reactions. Perceiving all thoughts, all feelings, and all behaviors as neutral are the key to letting them pass. If you believe there are good thoughts and bad thoughts, good feelings and bad feelings, how can you let the mental states you are in just pass? You will instead be stuck in grasping, resisting, or ignoring. Then the only answer is escapism.

There is an ancient story of an old farmer who had worked his crops for many years. One day his horse ran away. Upon hearing the news, his neighbors came to visit. "Such bad luck," they said sympathetically. "Maybe," the farmer replied. The next morning the horse returned, bringing with it three other wild horses. "How wonderful," the neighbors exclaimed. "Maybe," replied the old man. The following day, his son tried to ride one of the untamed horses, was thrown, and broke his leg. The neighbors again came to offer their sympathy for his misfortune. "Maybe," answered the farmer. The day after, military officials came to the village to draft young men into the army. Seeing that the son's leg was broken, they passed him by. The neighbors congratulated the farmer on how well things had turned out. "Maybe," said the farmer.

For many people, escapism is a way of life. I have worked with clients who keep themselves so busy from morning to night they do not have time to feel. They work and work and work, and often get involved with gossip and dramas about people in their life because they are fueling attachment and aversion while they ignore the rest of their deeper feelings. Human beings have been given the precious gift of being able to feel emotions and to use thoughts and feelings to enhance each moment of life as a continuous learning experience. We were born to learn, grow, thrive, and progress toward a greater version of ourselves as we share our existence with others. Many great teachers and enlightened masters have stated a human birth is rare and precious. If a person avoids presence and lives in the realm of distraction and escapism, how can his or her potential ever be realized?

Working in the mental health field, I have seen that escapism rules. It not only is a distraction technique, it becomes a goal for many people who suffer from stress overload. I have noticed the main reason people default to distraction and escapism is the present moment is being avoided. The present moment is too painful, too stressful, or too boring to pay attention to; the present is just not interesting enough. The past is much more interesting for people to immerse their attention. They identify with the past and get stuck there. Or, there are some who are so focused on the future, they forge ahead with a superficial euphoria about the life they are creating in their mind that may or may not manifest. Then there are those who take control of the present by covering it up with a distraction such as overworking, overindulging, alcohol and drug use, sex addiction, overspending, over-exercising, self-harm, and other unhealthy patterns. The ultimate escapism from this unhealthy perspective is suicide when life becomes so unbearable the person chooses a permanent solution.

If only the people who choose unhealthy distractions would be aware of the transitory nature of life, they may not continue to follow these unhelpful patterns. Whatever pain, suffering, uncomfortableness, or stress a person feels, it will pass. Just knowing this on an intellectual level is not enough; it must be experienced. Experiencing each moment fully, allows it to pass naturally. That is why distraction techniques cannot be the only coping strategies used for stress management. Using techniques that are based on the internal experience that everything comes and goes is the most helpful way to manage and prevent stress. Techniques such as nondirective meditation, yoga, tai chi, and music-sound therapy can cultivate an experience of being grounded and centered in the present, revealing the transient nature of existence. We will discuss these techniques in more detail as this book unfolds.

Whatever a person experiences, at any given time, will pass, and what comes next is part of the field of all possibilities. Being open to the unpredictability of life is a courageous way to live, and the best way to experience a genuine, honest, open existence. Be fully yourself without judgment; be in the present moment as it is; allow life to unfold. What is there to escape to? Only a one-sided existence that is not reality.

LSF Takeaway #8

Being fully aware of thoughts, feelings, and actions, experiencing them naturally, without distracting yourself, is the antidote to escapism. When life's responsibilities and interactions with others prevents you from fully experiencing your thoughts and feelings at that moment, it is important to find a way to process situations in order to metabolize the experience. To "digest" stressful experiences, talk about your thoughts and feelings with a trusted person: a friend, a family member, your neighbor, your spouse, or your therapist. If there is nobody to process your experience with, use journaling. The act of writing brings the situation out of your mind and body, to a neutral place where you can see your thoughts outside of yourself. This is a great way to metabolize experiences. Keep a paper journal, an electronic journal on your iPad or iPhone, or even an audio journal to record your thoughts and feelings. If you are an artist, draw or paint your feelings. These are all healthy ways to digest experiences.

CHAPTER 9

Exhaustion

n 1968, the Beatles recorded the song, "I'm So Tired," with lyrics that shared the experience of feeling so tired you can't sleep, can't think, don't know what to do, and are looking for peace of mind. I think it is safe to say the sentiments of this song are all too familiar. We overwork, overthink, over-feel, are overly tired, and eventually become "sick of it all." This is a disempowering state of mind and a sign that it is truly the age of exhaustion. Besides the ever-increasing demands of corporate America resulting in expanded work hours becoming the norm, there are many other responsibilities and activities that consume most people's weekly schedules. When you add up the hours worked for your job, the hours needed to take care of your family, the time required for upkeep of your home, the extra activities such as church meetings, volunteer work or social events, and trying to include exercise into the schedule — no wonder life has become so exhausting.

The words of F. Scott Fitzgerald, from his second novel The Beautiful and Damned, state: "Tired, tired with nothing, tired with everything, tired with the world's weight he had never chosen to bear." How many of us can relate to this feeling?

I recently met with a client who is an amazing asset to the company she works for. She has a great work ethic and prioritizes helping her team operate as efficiently as possible to best help her customers, putting in many extra hours to accomplish this. She added up her actual work hours for one week and was shocked to realize she works 60-80 hours per week. No wonder she has a tendency to get frustrated at home, has disturbed sleep, decreased appetite, and recently had a health issue requiring surgery. We were not meant to work this hard.

Since physical exhaustion is easy to understand — how it occurs and what it does to the body — this chapter will focus on mental exhaustion. When you use your mind intensely, whether you are trying to solve a problem, rehashing a situation to understand it, obsessing about an attachment or aversion, or concentrating too much on one thing, you will experience mental exhaustion. This is also a side effect of unrealistic educational expectations or the unreasonable demands for completing work responsibilities, depending on the type of school curriculum or job you are involved with.

Mental exhaustion first manifests as a mind you cannot shut off. All the mental focus you engaged in continues its processes even after you decide to stop thinking. The mind is on autopilot and it just keeps going. This is what keeps people up at night when trying to sleep. This is what interferes with being fully present at the moment while it is happening. This is what causes poor concentration, memory deficits, and an inability to make decisions. The mind cannot stop its incessant drive to concentrate on itself. It becomes a runaway train.

The next phase is "complete shutdown." The mind reaches its saturation point and your inability to be fully present and aware becomes overwhelming, leading to mental exhaustion. You literally cannot think anymore. At this point, the only thing you can do is rest and distract yourself. You become ineffective and uninspired. If this mindset happens on a regular basis, it is usually a sign your life is completely out of balance.

Whenever too much focus is put on one or two areas of life at the expense of the other areas, stress will occur. Whether it is intentional or unintentional does not matter. Balance in all things is the answer. If too much concentration is directed toward anything, whether it is work, school, relationships, or physical health, an imbalance will occur. This can lead to mental or physical exhaustion.

According to Living Stress Free, there are Eight Areas in each person's life that are universal:

1. Mental Health - your thoughts and feelings
2. Physical Health - diet, exercise, sleep, and self-care
3. Relationships - your spouse, family, friends, coworkers, professionals, etc.
4. Work/Contribution - paid or unpaid work and home tasks
5. Education - formal or informal learning
6. Recreation - anything you do purely for fun and enjoyment
7. Prosperity - finances, possessions, your "stuff" and what you do with it
8. Spirituality - connectedness and universal energy within and without of religion

The moment you start putting all of your focus and attention on only certain areas of your life, you will create an imbalance. The best way to avoid stress is to honor all of these Eight Areas regularly. There may not be time to pay attention to all of them each day, but increasing awareness of the areas being ignored and intentionally paying more attention to those areas as soon as possible will help prevent mental exhaustion. More details about the LSF Eight Areas will be discussed in Chapter Eighteen.

One of the hidden causes of mental exhaustion is trying too hard. The more intensely you try, the more you may struggle; struggle always leads to exhaustion. Trying is a misunderstood concept. We don't have to try really hard to figure something out. We have to stay alert and aware without the struggle. This is what going with the flow is all about. Ironically, when you go with the flow, the answers will often come naturally.

Imagine you are swimming in the ocean and a wave comes. Do you try and swim against the wave to navigate it? What would happen if you did? You would be knocked over. Instead, you go with the wave and allow it to carry you to the shore. Life is exactly like this. Approaching tasks with a sense of ease and calmness always brings a more complete result; you will solve the problem and maintain your sense of balance.

Another way you might unconsciously cause your own exhaustion is through purposely doing too much to avoid other parts of life that may be causing frustration, disappointment or discontent. This is another form of escapism. I used to have a neighbor who mowed his lawn for hours each weekend, making sure the lines were in perfect diagonal rows. His lawn was a work of art but it took so much time. He looked very tired by the end of the day. He was never seen with his spouse; instead, he was always working around the yard. A year later he separated from his wife and moved away. It may have been that he worked so much in order to avoid the other areas of his life that were unsatisfactory, which exhausted him.

A major "red flag" for mental exhaustion is misunderstanding effort. We are taught to put a lot of effort into everything we do. Teachers, coaches, and parents most likely told us: "You're not trying hard enough; you need to put more effort into it." Discipline and straining are valued in our society. However, there is another way of perceiving effort. A disciplined effort is often driven by an ulterior motive. Many of us try really hard to get a good grade, impress the boss, win the race, or make more money. Effort breeds extrinsic motivation which is behavior driven by external rewards. What if we replace effort with alert attention? Alert attention requires awareness and being fully present. All actions can be successfully performed in this state of alert awareness. Alert attention breeds intrinsic motivation: behavior driven by personal satisfaction and accomplishment. This creates a more balanced perspective.

Here are six suggestions to increase balance in your life and prevent exhaustion from slipping into your mind and body:

Sleep. Sleep is the most important way to prevent exhaustion. Sleep is the best antidote to stress. Sleep not only rests the nervous system, it helps you work out your stress in your dreams. It allows you to wake up with new perspectives and a clear mind. Restful sleep brings you back to your default state of effectiveness each and every day.

Value your Mental and Physical Health. There was a magnet on the refrigerator in my home growing up that stated: "Being good isn't good enough." I had a major dislike for that magnet because it was suggesting the only method to complete any action is through striving for perfection and excellence. If we feel we must always strive for perfection in everything we do we will inevitably lose our balance and become exhausted. It infers that there is more value attached to great achievement than there is to feeling happy, healthy, calm, and balanced. Be aware of what you truly value in life and adjust accordingly.

Beware of your Ego. There is a lot of pride connected with being a hard worker. People are impressed by hard workers. Once you identify as being someone who proudly works eighty-hour weeks, there is no hope for anything but exhaustion. Do not listen to ideas about whom you think you are. Look at the reality of who you are and how you actually feel. Beware of your extrinsic motivation vs intrinsic motivation.

Focus on Process, not Product. Performing your actions for the sake of the action itself and not the fruits of the action is an ancient practice called karma yoga. When this is practiced, you automatically are in the present moment as you do your task. For example, exercise just to exercise because it feels good to move. Drop the goal of losing twenty pounds or increasing muscle mass. When you are in sync with the action itself you will not exhaust yourself and the benefits will spontaneously occur because your focus is pure and undisturbed.

Balance the Scale. Balance requires awareness. First, you must become aware of over-concentration on some part of your life. Maybe you're thinking about someone too much, watching your diet excessively, or indulging your desire to watch Netflix all day. Be aware you are doing this, and then remind yourself to change it up and focus on another area of your life. It doesn't have to be anything monumental. You can honor education by looking something up on YouTube you want to learn more about. You can drive to a new park to walk around to honor physical health and recreation. You can attend to your possessions by cleaning out the junk drawer in your kitchen. Balance is the key to living optimally.

Practice Meditation Regularly. Nondirective meditation directly results in spontaneous awareness and balanced living. It is the fastest most effective way to honor your basic needs to live more effectively with improved health, happiness, and success. Even if your life is set up in a way that cultivates exhaustion and nothing can be changed right now, meditation will help tremendously. You can learn nondirective meditation in Chapter Sixteen, which offers full instructions for Living Stress Free Meditation.

LSF Takeaway #9

Mental exhaustion leads to stress reactions. If you have constant thoughts or an inability to think clearly, you may have mental fatigue. A lack of balance or putting too much focus on only a few areas of your life will often plant the seeds of mental and physical exhaustion. Review the six suggestions from this chapter whenever you begin to feel your mental fatigue settling in. Just these simple reminders will help you reverse the patterns that lead to stress-induced exhaustion.

CHAPTER 10

Velcro Past

We two kept house, the Past and I,
The Past and I;
I tended while it hovered nigh,
Leaving me never alone.
It was a spectral housekeeping
Where fell no jarring tone,
As strange, as still a housekeeping
As ever has been known.
— EXCERPT FROM "THE GHOST OF THE PAST"
BY THOMAS HARDY

The past is our companion as well as our nemesis. Our memories contain so much joy, sweetness, and beauty and at the same time so much heartbreak, frustration, and regret. There are incredible times and special people we want to remember the rest of our lives, and there are situations we would give our last penny to forget forever. The past haunts us, protects us, guides us, comforts us and bothers us endlessly. This is the human condition. But why?

The mind is a holding tank for memory; all thoughts are from the past. If you are a skeptic and want to prove this, take a piece of paper and put a timer on for two minutes. During that two minutes write down every thought you have. After the timer goes off review your thoughts. All of them are from past thoughts, feelings, and experiences. Even your plans and ideas about the future are based on the past because they are being filtered through your mental database of information about the future. If you walked into a completely new experience with no reference point from past knowledge, there would not be any thought about it. All thought is formed from past memories.

The problem is not that our minds are filled with only memories. The problem is most people are not aware of this fact. We become fascinated with past thoughts, feelings, and experiences. Fondly remembering something is one thing, but wishing you can go back is another.

The American musical duo, Twenty One Pilots, released a song in 2015 entitled "Stressed Out," with lyrics describing the transition from adolescence to adulthood and the desire to "turn back time to the good ol' days." The truth is there is only now, there is only the present. When people are drawn to the past they are intentionally directing their focus away from the present moment. This occurs for many reasons. Maybe the present isn't all that interesting. Maybe the present is too difficult or too disturbing. Dwelling on the past is a common distraction technique and a form of escapism.

There are also those who unintentionally think about the past. For these folks, there is something about the past that is not understood, unresolved, or unsettled. Feelings accompany this tendency to ruminate about the past, usually in the form of guilt, shame, anger, or regret. Sometimes contemplating the past will help it be understood, especially if a person is sharing it with a close friend or their therapist.

Sometimes the past will never be understood. That is when the only solution is to drop the why. Asking why something occurred will rarely produce an answer that is satisfactory. Dropping the incessant "why" is one secret to letting go and moving on. If a person cannot stop asking why they are often identified as being a victim of or contributor to the situation in some way. Either way, the only answer is to direct attention to the present moment as often as possible.

Velcro is a brand name for a special cloth material having two rough surfaces that stick together when pressed. The past can be like Velcro if the person's attention is restless and not grounded in the present moment. If you can't be in the here and now the only place to go is to the past. The past lives in the mind, not in reality. Holding onto past relationships in your mind, whether they are positive or negative, leads to living outside of reality, dwelling in the fascination of your ideas. This is the reason so many people live in their head and have difficulty paying attention, listening, remembering, and concentrating. The Velcro past is very sticky.

The Velcro past is a breeding ground for cultivating anger, resentment, depression, guilt, grief, obsessions, and addiction. It is the main ingredient of stress. The more a person lives from the filter of the past, the more identified they will be with their ideas from the past, unaware these are their ideas based on their personal experiences and not necessarily reality. Reality is in the present, constantly unfolding with new experiences, new situations, and new interactions. Life is a fascinating journey that is ever fresh, ever new, for one who can ride the wave of the present moment and break the Velcro ties in their mind.

Imagine how transformed your life could be if you let go of the past. Here's an exercise to see what it feels like. Think about the past three months and the places you went to. See if you can recall a brand new place you experienced, whether it was a restaurant, park, store, coffee shop, or classroom. In the moment of experiencing something new, you had nothing to give you security or familiarity. This may have felt a little scary. However, on the other hand, there was an excitement, a curiosity, a spark of freshness. You were completely dwelling in the reality of the moment, not your ideas about the moment. How did that feel?

About fifteen years ago, part of my responsibilities at the mental health clinic I work for was to take the clients on outings to expand their recreational experiences. One particular Friday, in August, we went to the local amusement park with an extensive water park. I had never been to a water park; this was a brand new experience for me. I still remember climbing up the steep staircase to the top of the waterslide which was called The Vortex. It was an enclosed tube that twisted and turned, with no way to actually see where it went unless you went through it. My mind began activating fearful memories. I am not a good swimmer and I started wondering if the tube dumped me into deep water, what would I do? What if it had very steep drops inside the tube? My stomach would have that uneasy feeling and there would be nothing I could do. I felt myself getting more anxious as the minutes dragged on. I almost turned around and went back down the stairs! None of this was reality; these were all thoughts based on memory. Finally, it was my turn to go down the tube and because at that moment I had no expectations to base the experience, it was amazingly fun! I let go and just enjoyed the ride. My mind literally shut off.

That is what letting go does: it allows you to enjoy life as it is, not how you think it is. Life will pleasantly surprise you most of the time; the times it doesn't will be over with before you know it. Time heals. Time helps you not get stuck. Time reminds you that the past is literally over and you cannot go back. As the Rolling Stones sang, "Time is on my side, yes it is."

Now that we've looked at the dangers of dwelling in the past too much, it becomes more obvious how unhealthy patterns are born out of this habit. Addiction is completely based on repeating past behaviors to secure a familiar result. Obsessive-compulsive disorder is a complete byproduct of going over the past repeatedly to create a sense of security. Post-traumatic stress disorder is defined by an inability for the body and mind to let go of the past because of the intensity of the trauma. Anxiety disorders are driven by worry based on comparing the past to the unknown future. Even hoarding is an attachment to the past. People who cannot throw anything out are clinging to memories to fill an emptiness that their "stuff" temporarily fills to solidify the past.

What do all of these examples have in common? Grasping the familiar for a sense of security, and a lack of trust in the present. Just like traveling down The Vortex, the way to embrace the reality of the present is through trust. Dive into the past for information, indulgence or sentimentality, but keep one foot in the present at all times.

LSF Takeaway #10

If you can remember that your mind's job is to create thought and that all your thoughts are entirely based on the past, you can see how it's easy to get drawn back to remembering the past and missing out on the present. This tendency interferes with living a happy, healthy life where the present feels fulfilling and enjoyable.

To get unstuck from the past, drop the need to ask why and just move on. Cultivate fascination with the present. Make it a habit to try something new next time you go out to eat. Intentionally take a new route home as you drive away from work or school. Listen to a new radio station just to change it up a little. Each new experience that you allow in your life will build trust in the unknowing. Life will then become a fascinating journey, more interesting than any memory from your Velcro past.

CHAPTER 11
Annihilate the Worrywart

n the 2015 Cold War thriller, "Bridge of Spies," James Donovan, a Brooklyn lawyer, asks Rudolf Abel, a convicted spy, "Do you never worry?" Abel replies, "Would it help?"

This answer stayed with me for months after I saw the movie because it has so much truth in it. Does worrying ever help? After working for years with anxious clients, as well as my own self-examination, I have to say with complete certainty — absolutely not.

Remember, the mind generates thoughts that are completely based on past experiences. The mind is only memory. The mind is like a computer hard drive with a lot of ram. When you think about the past, you are sorting through old files that create emotions. The past can make you feel proud, loved, uplifted, or it can lead to guilt, sadness, regret or anger. These files unlock doors of emotion when they are opened. It can be like releasing "Pandora's box" at times! If you ponder this truism it could make you think twice about getting lost in thought during idle moments or sleepless nights. It isn't your mind doing this to you; it is your decision to access your mind.

When you are taking in new information in the present moment, your mind is creating new files simultaneously; it is an automatic process. Your eyes are a camera, your ears are a recorder, and all of your senses are taking in data to store in your mind-body. Once you review the information you took in, you are back in the past. It is a completely mechanical, systematic process. The mind is the greatest computer ever designed. Reviewing the stored information in your mind can be extremely helpful in deductive reasoning, planning and strategizing, solving problems, and setting goals. This information allows you to succeed in school, present an amazing work demonstration, and remember your lines while acting in a play on stage. It is this mechanical process that makes us uniquely human.

What about the times you worry about the future? The future is not here yet. There is no way of knowing what will happen in the future, with any real certainty. Look at your own life and you will see it. How many times has the course of events that occurred in your life been nothing like you imagined? Uncertainty is a reality. Every time you worry about the future, what are you basing it on? The past and the past is a warehouse of accumulated memories. You are never accurately thinking about the future because this is impossible; the future has not yet arrived to have any experience of. You are speculating about the future based on the past. This realization is the first step to changing your relationship with anxiety.

Anxiety, nervousness, fear, worry, and apprehension are all emotions that stem from the incorrect notion that just because something happened in the past to you or someone else, it will happen again to you in the future. Where did you get this information? Prophetic dreams? A personal psychic? A crystal ball? No matter what anyone tells you, no matter what the statistics say or what the scientists warn you, you do not know for sure what will happen in the future. You are a unique individual with an individual destiny. There are just as many stories of people who beat the odds, succeeded when they "should have" failed, or prevailed despite it all, as there are examples of those who ended up as expected. No matter what anyone tells you, you cannot say with any certainty what the reason is for these different results. Given that, Rudolph Abel's remark "would it help?" to the question of worry is an excellent answer.

So now that you know your mind is the reason you get stuck in fear reactions, why can't you just stop this pattern? If it was that easy the world would be a very different place. Anxiety and fear are the root causes of all conflict and strife. If you analyze fear it often comes from an "us and them" mentality. You feel separate from someone or something. The opposite of the feeling of fear is the feeling of love. Love and fear cannot exist at the same time. That is why prayer helps many people who feel scared. It is an immediate antidote to feeling separate and alone. That is also why there have always been some people who cannot be alone. Their fear factor is just too strong.

Another reason the tendency to feel separate from others is rampant is the judgmental mind. The mind loves to compare and judge, deciding this is good and this is bad, this is right and this is wrong. Once there is polarization there is separation. This leads to fear and anxiety. Where did these ideas to have judgments come from? They came from past impressions from the database of the mind.

Probably the most common reason anxiety and worry become cultivated in the mind is that many people are uncomfortable with not knowing. The future is uncertain and everyone knows this deep down inside. There are some people who are fine with not knowing. These people have spent a lot of time in the present moment living mindfully. But for others, uncertainty is scary. They would rather cling to ideas not based on reality than face not knowing. There is a common tendency to try and know what will happen in any given situation, but there is no truth in knowing the future. The best you can do is have an educated guess, allowing for the inevitable uncertainty factor, but remain open and ready for whatever unfolds.

Often the need to know what will happen in the future is an inherent need for control. Allowing for not knowing means the person is able to let go of control, with the ability to just see what happens. For many people, control is extremely important in life and it is difficult to refrain from this need and just go with the flow.

To illustrate just how powerful the mind's past impressions affect reality, here are three examples of debilitating problems that occur as a result of worrywart mentality.

Obsessive Compulsive Disorder

People who struggle with OCD have an incessant need to check something over and over, whether it's a thought they need reassurance about or a physical action they need to repeat to make sure it was done correctly. If you analyze the process the mind is engaged in with this pattern, it becomes clear the source is an inability to fully pay attention to the present moment. If a person with OCD is fully aware and not interacting with their ideas and their mind that is filled with past impressions, they would know they said or did the proper response. OCD is a result of one who is too lost in thought. It manifests as the mind's way of paying attention after the action was completed, which only engages the mind more. Since the mind is only memory, the memory of uncertainty leaves the person in an endless state of worry. It also can result from the tendency to over-concentrate on one thing to the exclusion of everything else. The person inevitably misses out on the present moment due to an inability to have inclusive awareness.

Performance Anxiety

Performance anxiety is the quintessential example of anticipatory anxiety. Ironically, the term anticipatory anxiety is actually redundant, because all anxiety is based on anticipation. Performance anxiety is a tendency to project fear into the future. As discussed earlier, fear is only based on the past, not the reality of now. Without the knowledge and experience of how to change attention from the thought realm to the experience of the present, there will be minimal relief.

As a musician, I can relate to this very much. I still recall standing on stage in front of my elementary school, playing my flute solo in the fifth grade. I was doing great, feeling great, and enjoying the sound of my flute. Then, like an unwelcome guest, the thought entered my mind "what if you make a mistake?" That was it. The shaking and sweating started, my breathing became shallow (not a helpful response for a flute player) and my playing suffered. What caused it? My mind and the attention on a thought that was not based on reality.

Memory Problems

If a person is lost in thought they are not fully present. The result? An inability to remember what just happened, what was just said, or what was just seen.

It starts out innocently enough. Then, in time, the person starts feeling bad about not remembering. This creates a deeper impression or groove in the mind that reinforces identification with not remembering. Thinking about life as opposed to experiencing life takes everyone out of the reality of the present moment.

A great example of this is when you join a group of people and everyone says their name. How often do you remember all their names? Not very often. Why? Because your mind started thinking about something, most likely how you will remember their names, and it blocked out alert attention to hear all the names. We all do this. A lack of awareness in the present causes memory deficits. This lack of awareness can be a result of dullness of attention, over-concentration, or fascination with internal thoughts.

As you can see from these examples, the mind's difficulty with remaining fully present leads to all kinds of secondary issues that increase stress and lead to unwelcome emotional reactions. The mind also creates a reality based on past impressions that are often tainted with judgments, assumptions, and false security. Thich Nhat Hanh, the Vietnamese Buddhist monk, once wrote: "Anxiety, the illness of our time, comes primarily from our inability to dwell in the present moment."

Try this experiment: Sit in a room by yourself, with no television, music, or computer to distract you. Where does your attention go? For most people, it will go to their thoughts — identification and attachment to thinking. You will sit there and think. Your thoughts will become more interesting than your environment. Even if the television, music or computer is on, many times your thoughts will still be more interesting than what is in your environment at that moment. With so much interest in the inner world of thinking, it becomes a perfect breeding ground for worry, anxiety, and fear to grow and expand. Thoughts keep you company and sow the seeds of your emotional reactions.

This is why I differentiate between distraction techniques and mindfulness techniques. Distraction techniques provide temporary relief from the thinking mind. They override the tendency to overthink. These include watching television, playing video games, going for a drive, sports, coloring, puzzles, crafts, exercise, etc. The list is endless and all are worthy distractions to prevent the mind from overthinking. They create an activity that is more interesting than the thoughts in the mind. However, when the activity is over it is very easy to go right back to thinking. It is a temporary solution.

Mindfulness techniques are designed to change the pattern of attachment to thinking by perceiving thoughts differently. Instead of focusing on what the thoughts are about, you perceive your thoughts as passing vibrations of energy, bubbles floating by, as discussed in Chapter Three. For example, if you put a radio station on in your car with a person sharing their political ideas, it would be natural to listen to what the person is saying. However, if you put a radio station on with a person speaking another language, you would not get drawn to the details of the conversation because you could not understand it. You no longer heard words, but sound. Watching your own thoughts as sound vibrations keep you out of the details of the thoughts. Other examples of mindfulness techniques include LSF Meditation which is a form of nondirective meditation, yoga, and internal martial arts. The methods for some of these practices will be discussed later in this book.

How can you get rid of anxiety? How can you annihilate the worrywart within? If you increase your awareness of the pattern that sews the seeds of anxiety, worry, and fear, you have the ability to change it. You cannot get rid of your thoughts, you cannot stop thinking, but you can change your relationship with your thoughts so they do not produce an emotional reaction. This is what I call "add, don't subtract." Notice your worry thoughts, remember they are not based on reality, and add more of the present moment to your experience. Add your breathing, your physical body, sounds in the environment, and physical sensations, while you notice your thoughts. You will no longer identify as a worrywart, but as a person having a moment filled with a variety of experiences.

The late comedian Gilda Radner, one of the great comic geniuses of the 20th century, has been quoted: "I wanted a perfect ending. Now I've learned, the hard way, that some poems don't rhyme, and some stories don't have a clear beginning, middle, and end. Life is about not knowing, having to change, taking the moment and making the best of it, without knowing what's going to happen next. Delicious Ambiguity."

LSF Takeaway #11

The future is filled with all possibilities and there is no way to know for sure what will happen. Using your mind to predict the future can be problematic and misleading because the mind is just a database of the past.

Here are two ways to help decrease anxiety and annihilate the worrywart, available to try right now:

1. Focus on Love - Whenever your mind is generating a fear reaction or uncertainty about the future, choose to think about someone or something you love. Fear cannot exist when you feel love.
2. Add, Don't Subtract - Open your awareness to what you are experiencing in addition to your thoughts and feelings: feel your body, hear sounds, smell aromas, notice your breathing. Inclusive awareness immediately leads to a mindful experience of the present moment which is an antidote to worry and anxiety.

CHAPTER 12
The Age of Rage

Growing up as a practicing Catholic, I remember having to go to confession. When I was a young girl I would ask my mother what I should say to the priest because I couldn't think of any sins to confess. She told me to confess to the priest if I felt angry since my last confession. I wondered to myself, "Anger is a sin?" That's what I was told. I don't blame my mother for this crazy dogma. She is a wonderful, loving person who tries to follow what she was taught and lives her life being thoughtful and kind to others. But the truth is that many people from different religions, separate socioeconomic brackets, and varied lifestyles believe that anger is bad, anger is wrong, and that anger is a sin. This belief is far from the truth, from my personal and professional experience, and from the perspective of Living Stress Free.

Whether you believe anger is a sin or not, it seems apparent we are living in the age of rage. There is no escaping it. Turn on the television and whether you are watching the news, sitcoms, reality shows, or movies, you will be watching angry people saying and doing angry things. Social media is filled with everyday folks sounding off about their strong opinions for this and against that. There is anger on the roads, in stores, at work, at concerts, in schools, and it doesn't even matter what age the person is. From mass shootings to bullying, and even in politics, there is much anger expressed.

Anger is an emotion everybody has felt. This is a fact. It is created within ourselves as a result of a thought or experience that created a reaction. If we don't judge this reaction as bad or negative we will feel it as energy. Anger is a burst of energy that is responding to something. Energy is energy; it is not good or bad. The more we can experience the "is-ness" of anger, the less we will fall into the trap of becoming attached to it, having an aversion to it, or ignoring it. As we learned in Chapter Five's "Pet the Cat," it helps tremendously to acknowledge the anger, allow it to be there, and continue with our moment to moment existence. The anger will feel validated and dissipate on its own. Since anger is energy it will pass as energy does.

Letting go of anger is challenging for many of us. If anger is acknowledged and allowed to be experienced, it takes approximately twenty minutes for anger to subside on its own, if it's not fed. Much like the premise of the 1984 movie Gremlins, in which you cannot feed the cute little creatures after midnight or else "all hell breaks loose," you cannot feed anger or it becomes a potential monster of energy. Feeding anger is thinking about what is causing the anger. Going over the details contributing to your anger causes the anger to stay right where it is: in your thoughts and feelings. Worse yet, if you act on your anger, it will prolong it and intensify the anger even more.

There are three reasons we feed our anger:

1. We want to find a solution to what we are angry about.
2. We want to solidify our opinion about what is making us angry.
3. We like to feel angry and want to stay that way.

All of these reasons take your focus out of the present and place it in your mind which is a container of the past. You lose out on life as it continues to unfold because of grasping the issues that caused the anger. Let's explore these three reasons in more detail.

Reason #1

What if you are looking to find a solution to a situation you are angry about? This is a natural response. If it's a new issue that has you frustrated, allow yourself the time to process it either through your own contemplation, talking to someone about it, or writing about it. Processing the issue is similar to digesting your food: it will help you metabolize your anger. Once you come up with a strategy, put it into action and move on with your life. If it's an old issue, it most likely is something you never had a chance to metabolize in the past. It is like undigested food sitting in your tissues and organs. The best strategy, in this case, is to work with a therapist or counselor to release the issue, if possible. If it cannot be resolved, you must "drop the why" and let it go.

Reason #2

What if you are reinforcing your opinion about something you feel strongly about? This tendency is very prevalent now, with much stress over the political situation in this country. Remember that opinion is based on a belief which is completely on the level of thought. All thoughts are from the past. By grasping your opinions and pushing them out onto others, you are draining your energy and reinforcing the past. Life is constantly moving forward and the future is filled with many possibilities. There is so much you do not know coming from the bigger picture of reality. Reinforcing opinions just reinforces the ego. Identification with being right about something is divisive. If possible, the best strategy is to state your thoughts and then move on to other parts of your life to keep yourself balanced. You never know what course of events will happen to bring change that is beyond your scope of awareness.

Another aspect that is prevalent when you overly promote strong opinions about certain issues or people is the "smoke and mirrors" effect. Oftentimes, people who spout off their opinions about what should or shouldn't be happening in society are projecting their anger onto social issues as a safe outlet to release frustration. The real anger and irritation may be connected to their personal life that they cannot, or will not, change or acknowledge. It's like the magician who is skilled at making the audience look on one side of the stage so they don't see where the real trick is occurring on the other side of the stage. This is the "smoke and mirrors" effect.

Reason #3

What if you are identified with your anger as part of you? Being angry is your go-to. Ask yourself: "Am I happy feeling angry?" Do you actually like feeling that way? Chances are you're not happy this way, but feel like you have no choice. Anger depletes you and takes away that which sustains you, especially over time. It has been linked to diseases such as cancer and heart attacks. However, the more you hold onto anger and make it a permanent guest in your mind and body, the more it will feel comfortable and familiar. Then you will worry whenever you are happy that you will inevitably be thrown back to anger because something will go wrong, again! This thinking is coming from the past, not the reality of the present. The present offers many possibilities. The best strategy to counteract this is to focus more on doing things than thinking about things.

It may cross your mind to ask: "You say I would benefit from letting it go, but I want a resolution." If you feel this way, know that it is the stress talking. The less stress you feel, the more you will be able to let things go. Stress loves resistance; stress thrives on conflict. The best strategy is to practice mindfulness methods, calming techniques, and activities that release your stress to prepare your mind to let things go. Be careful of distraction techniques such as watching television, enjoying an alcoholic beverage, or working out at the gym. They only provide temporary relief but the issue will remain. Distraction is best used when you feel intense anger and you need to bring it down a few notches quickly.

The most lethal form of anger that can destroy the mind, body, and soul is resentment. Resentment spreads like cancer and is very difficult to extract. Resentment is defined as bitter indignation from being treated unfairly. It is so powerful because most of the time the person feeling resentment is totally justified and correct. Holding onto the validation of feeling justified through the resentment helps the person feel like they are making up for the wrongs that were done to them. It is the ego wanting to be justified. The ego is dwelling in the past and reinforcing the past to feel more secure and comforted, but resentment and bitterness do not feel good at all! The late Carrie Fisher is quoted as saying, "Resentment is like taking poison and waiting for the other person to die." Avoid resentment like the plague. The antidote? Focus on what you do have right now, not on what you don't have.

Anger can be increased through other factors besides life circumstances and ruminating thoughts. A lack of restful sleep can lead to irritability, annoyance, and a "short fuse." If you try to get through the day without proper rest you can be set off by small events that normally would not bother you. Physical pain often leads to frustration and anger. Alcohol consumption and some types of recreational drug use can cause anger and rage. Some foods have a tendency to spike irritability, such as spicy foods, according to Ayurveda, an ancient form of medicine described in the Vedic scriptures of India. Hormone and blood sugar imbalances lead to irritability as well. The most cleverly disguised form of anger is anxiety. Anxiety and worry may be the real issue but they can be expressed as anger. Sometimes a chronically angry person is actually a very worried, nervous individual underneath.

There is a wonderful benefit to anger: energy. Energy helps you accomplish tasks, it enables you to exercise, it is motivating. Energy gets you out of a rut. Have you ever experienced being in a situation that seems like it will never end, or it will never get better? Maybe it's a room in your house that you need to clean out and it just keeps getting piled up with more junk. Over time it becomes more and more disorganized and unable to use. You walk by it every day and don't even want to go in. One day you get so frustrated and angry about it, you burst into the room with a huge lawn and leaf garbage bag and start throwing everything out. What happened? Anger gave you the energy to change the pattern that was filled with inertia. This same force can pull you out of depression as well.

LSF Takeaway #12

The more you can move away from designating your thoughts and emotions as good or bad, the less stress you will feel. Anger is not good or bad. It is useful at times and helps increase awareness of how to thrive in this world. Use the energy from anger to help you. However, beware of grasping, resisting, or ignoring anger. Acknowledge and validate the anger, then allow it to pass. Put your attention on the next task at the next moment, instead of going over the details of what you are angry or frustrated about.

CHAPTER 13

Can You Truly Be Happy?

The United States Declaration of Independence states that all citizens have the right to "Life, Liberty and the Pursuit of Happiness." Happiness is listed as one of the top three values that this country is based on. What strikes me about this statement though, is it says the "pursuit" of happiness, not the attainment of happiness. Meaning, if you live in the US you have the right to try and be happy but there is no guarantee you will be.

After contemplating happiness in my own life and in my work with others who are seeking it, I can say with absolute certainty that happiness is not something to achieve — it is our birthright. Happiness is already within each of us. If something makes us feel happy, it is not the object of our attention creating this feeling. The source of happiness is coming from within. The object of our attention that triggered this reaction is just a mirror showing what is already there, giving the optimal circumstance to let it shine.

The idea of pursuing happiness is a waste of energy when looking at it from this perspective. Why pursue something you already have? The pursuit of happiness for many people becomes their life mission and they are identified with *trying* to get there. When do they get to feel happy? Do they struggle and toil to attain this goal and expect to feel incredibly happy forever after? It seems more logical, practical, and efficient to uncover the hidden gem of happiness that we are walking around with every day. We already have it and we can access it anytime we want.

In the 1939 movie, The Wizard of Oz, Glinda the Good Witch tells Dorothy: "You don't need to be helped any longer. You've always had the power to go back to Kansas."

The Scarecrow says, "Then why didn't you tell her before?"

Glinda says, "She wouldn't have believed me. She had to learn it for herself."

Scarecrow asks Dorothy, "What have you learned?"

Dorothy says: "If I ever go looking for my heart's desire again, I won't look any further than my own backyard. Because if it isn't there, I never really lost it, to begin with!"

Dorothy learned the secret to happiness. She did not have to pursue it, it was already there.

What is stopping you from feeling happy right now? Since it is already inside, there must be "stuff" that is covering it up, right? I've had clients tell me they cannot even remember the last time they felt happy. That is how much the feeling of happiness can be obliterated by stressors. Other clients have told me they used to have long periods of time when they experienced happiness, and then the happiness disappeared, causing a huge loss and a strong desire to get the feeling back. The ever-elusive happiness has become a goal for many and an attainment for few, it seems. Even people with lots of money, possessions, success, and status are found to be unhappy despite their attainment. Some of them go so far as to end their life, as in the recent cases of Anthony Bourdain and Kate Spade. This only proves happiness is not based on achievement, but rather an inner state that confirms everything is the way it is at that moment, and that is fine.

Finding a definition of happiness is also an elusive task. Try it sometime! There are the philosophical meanings, the psychological definitions, and even religious ideas on the description of this emotion. The Merriam-Webster dictionary defines happiness as "a state of well-being and contentment; a pleasurable or satisfying experience." Other definitions I found include the qualities of good fortune and prosperity.

From the perspective of being a mindfulness practitioner as well as a long-term mental health therapist, this is how I perceive happiness: it is transitory, just like everything else. This does not denote a negative perspective; it is just a fact. Every thought, feeling, experience, physical sensation, and breath comes into our awareness and passes eventually. There is nothing that is permanent except for awareness itself.

For example, if you have a thought that you feel ignored by your coworkers, that thought will last while you entertain it, but it will eventually go away. The feeling of sadness or anger about being ignored will also go away in time, especially if you put your focus on something else. If your coworkers decide to make you the employee of the month the next day at work, and you feel valued and appreciated, that feeling of happiness will also drift away over the course of time.

Happiness *about* something is not sustainable; happiness based on an idea cannot be maintained. Happiness is a feeling that will pass just like anger or sadness. The true attainment is contentment. Contentment leads to happiness but happiness does not always lead to contentment. The definition of contentment is a state of happiness and satisfaction. It is not a feeling; it is a state of mind. It is far greater than happiness because contentment can be a state of mind one can live life from.

When you explore the definition of contentment from the Urban Dictionary, an online resource for slang words and phrases, it states contentment is "true peace of mind and has nothing to do with any external pleasure or condition, but rather your attitude." It is not possible to live life in a happy mood all the time. When one tries, it can become forced, contrived, and even annoying to others. Living life with a sense of contentment and satisfaction will not only help you thrive, it will help those around you thrive as well.

What is stopping you from feeling contentment? Here are seven observations on this subject based on my experiences with myself and others.

1. **Identification with being an unhappy person.** There are those who are so used to things not going their way, or circumstances not working out, that they start to expect this as reality. This is the quintessential self-fulfilling prophecy. It becomes their very sense of self and they would not know who they are if they were happy. It

is too unfamiliar. The only answer to this dilemma is the awareness that this pattern is happening and shifting identification to other aspects of their self, expanding perspective.

2. **Basing happiness on thoughts and ideas instead of experiences.** This is a very common pattern. So many people live in their head and have a strong ideology about how things should be and what has to happen. There is no room for other perspectives, spontaneity, and open-mindedness. Whenever anyone is obsessed with right and wrong, good and bad, or us and them thinking patterns, there is no room for openness, flexibility, and contentment. Making decisions based on thoughts and ideas about life instead of the reality of the situation leads to poor decision making, a lack of lasting satisfaction, and mood making, which is a temporary elated feeling resulting from lofty thinking. It cannot be sustained. Happiness cannot be derived from thinking alone; it thrives on experiences.

3. **Seriousity.** Although not commonly used, the word means being too serious all the time. Serious people may be well-intentioned, but they never seem happy. One of the qualities of successfully content, joyful people is their light-hearted nature. They have the ability to see the humor in most situations and never take themselves too seriously. The ego thrives on seriousness. The ego is never content.

4. **Desire and resistance.** Desire, attachment, and clinging to the things we want, will lead to dissatisfaction because we can never get everything we want. Resistance, aversion, and trying to get rid of things we don't want also lead to frustration because we can never get rid of everything we dislike. Focusing on what we don't have instead of what we do have is a toxic habit. The best solution is to stop wanting to feel happy and let yourself feel as you feel, allowing what is to be as it is. Contentment and happiness can sometimes come solely through surrender and acceptance.

5. **Too much stress.** Stress, from the LSF perspective, is anything interfering with our needs, causing an imbalance. Stress is synonymous with unhappiness. Even the people who say they love stress may not be truly happy. They are charged with their ideas about what

they want to attain. Stress puts a damper on happiness. Sometimes the best solution is to manage and decrease stress by finding the balance in life and changing your relationship with stress. Happiness and contentment will have a better chance of showing up.

6. **Not enjoying your own company.** Whether this comes from poor self-esteem, feelings of worthlessness, trauma, or boredom, like it or not you are stuck with yourself. The antidote to this disempowerment is to understand who you really are. If you think you are the sum total of your past experiences, mistakes, and people's impressions of you, you are not seeing the bigger picture of who you are. If you only feel good about yourself when you accomplish something, you will be at risk for dissatisfaction throughout your life. There is much more to discover and awareness is the path to get there.

7. **Being addicted to extreme emotions.** Some people only feel alive when they are feeling, and they think something is missing if they don't feel emotions intensely. These are the drama seekers who indulge emotions. This always leads to being out of balance and inevitably increases stress. Valuing contentment is the first step to changing this destructive pattern.

Nobody is happy all the time. Even the great beings that have graced the world with their teachings and presence, such as Jesus, Buddha, Krishna, Moses, and a myriad of saints, sages, and healers, were not happy all the time. Human beings are supposed to feel different emotions on a regular basis. There is nothing wrong with that. We don't need to take medication to fix this unless the emotions get stuck too long in one area disrupting the ability to function. Our feelings and emotions are much like the weather: always changing. If we perceive the weather from the eye of awareness, we know it will pass. In the same way, awareness tells us our feelings will pass as well.

Can you truly be happy? Yes, happiness is found through awareness and contentment. One of my favorite poems about awareness and contentment was recited by Edward Espe Brown in a 2007 movie called "How To Cook Your Life" filmed at the Tassajara Mountain Center and San Francisco Zen Center. It is a perfect way to wrap up this chapter.

The Little Duck

Now we are ready to look at something pretty special.
It is a duck riding the ocean a hundred feet beyond the surf,
And he cuddles in the swells.
There is a big heaving in the Atlantic.
And he is part of it.
He can rest while the Atlantic heaves,
because he rests in the Atlantic.
Probably he doesn't know how large the ocean is.
And neither do you.
But he realizes it.
And what does he do, I ask you.
He sits down in it.
He reposes in the immediate as if it
were infinity – which it is.
That is religion, and the duck has it.
I like the little duck.
He doesn't know much.
But he has religion.
DONALD BABCOCK, *THE LYFE POEMS OF DONALD BABCOCK*

LSF Takeaway #13

The answer to the ever-elusive pursuit of happiness is to seek contentment. Contentment is cultivated through awareness of what is and experiencing the present moment fully. Whatever emotions and feelings occur in the present moment, allow yourself to experience them fully. Only then will you be truly alive, not missing any moment of time in your lifespan. This leads to fulfillment and satisfaction. As John Lennon wrote in his song Beautiful Boy: "Life is what happens to you while you're busy making other plans." He was referring to missing out on the present moment when you are lost in your thinking about ideas of life. Contentment is a feeling of fulfillment that only occurs when you are living life, not functioning from your ideas about life.

CHAPTER 14

Getting Out of Your Own Way

Ever ask yourself, "Why can't I just do it?" Whether it is starting a new diet, exercising, registering for an online course, or working on updating your resume, making a change is not always smooth and easy. You might have great goals with logical reasons for making a change, but something always seems to get in the way, doesn't it? This chapter is devoted to getting you out of your own way because the "something" that seems to get in the way is usually YOU.

I never set goals. Goals come with baggage. The Merriam-Webster dictionary defines the word goal as "an end toward which effort is directed." When there is effort there will most likely be stress. An effort is often required in life but so is letting go and allowing nature to take its course. Effort without flexibility results in tension. Life is about balance: balancing self-effort and discipline with awareness of what nature is teaching you. When I use the word "nature" I am referring to the situations and circumstances that naturally occur in life that you have no control over. I stated that goals come with baggage because pushing through natural resistances to achieve what you want gives the ego too much power. Living by the ego alone interferes with happiness, health, and fulfillment, the key components of a successful, stress-free life.

The ego is the sum total of all your past impressions from your life's experiences. It is the false reality of whom you think you are. It tells you what you like, what you don't like, what should happen, and how life is supposed to be. It compares you to others and finds fault in life when it doesn't give you what you want. It is the home base for desire and resistance. It gets you in trouble all the time. It makes you have hurt feelings, it supports your addictions, it gives you false confidence, and it tells you negative things about yourself and others. It creates stories about people and things not based on reality but purely based on your ideas about reality. Your belief system is coming from your ego. The ego is formed by past impressions, so it has nothing to do with being in the present moment, living mindfully, and experiencing *now* without commentary. The ego is the force behind setting a goal and struggling with it when you have challenges along the way. It knocks off your balance, which increases stress. This is the baggage I'm referring to.

Instead of setting goals, I set intentions. Intentions are defined as "what a person intends to do or bring about based on determination and resolve." Intention is direction without grasping. It is a more balanced perspective on moving toward the desired result. An intention is not driven by the ego, which is the seat of desire. An intention has a focused but flexible trajectory that allows for the support of nature. To use a photography metaphor, a goal would be zooming in to a point of reference and an intention would be using a wide angle lens and zooming out towards the general direction you want to capture.

An example that may help differentiate the attitudinal shift between goals and intentions happened to me recently. I have one room in my house that has become the storage area for anything I don't have a place for, items I need to decide to save or throw out, or things I'm too busy to put back where they belong. I'm sure some of you have a similar room in your house. The room is a mess, frustrating both me and my husband to the extent we don't even want to go in it. In the past, I tried to set a goal to enter the room weekly, taking one item at a time, putting it where it belongs or throwing it out. Did I ever achieve this goal? No. Why? Because I felt stress just thinking about it and I was avoiding that feeling of stress. It was too overwhelming. I had better things to do with my time. However, I set an intention this year to reclaim the room. Circumstances naturally came together for me to take some time off to tackle the room, which I did. Did I cause those circumstances to come together? Partially, but I allowed for life to intervene and show me the best time to do it. I was open to the signs I was given due to the practice of being in the present moment each day and experiencing life as it unfolds instead of my ideas about what should be. Awareness is the key to successful change.

Let's get back to how you might be getting in your own way of setting intentions. Have you wanted to make a healthy change in your life but can't seem to get started? In my work with helping people change their life, I have found the following six reasons as common barriers demonstrating how people get in their own way.

Reason 1 - Fascination with Ideas

Some people have no intention of following through with something they want to change, but they enjoy the idea of it. For example, I have friends who like the idea of becoming a vegan, but they have resistance to putting it into practice because the reality of the situation is they would not be able to eat a strict diet such as that with the influence of their spouse and children who love to eat meat and dairy. There are other people who are filled with lots of ideas. They get excited by all the things they want to do and often tell you all the things that you could do. This is what's known as mood making. The ideas make them feel excited because thoughts lead to feelings, but there is no depth or follow through; no action is taken. Before you can change or problem-solve anything, you need to be aware of what's possible given the actual circumstances of right now, not your ideas of right now. Form intentions based on reality, not ideas.

Reason 2 - Stuck in Thoughts, Feelings, and Emotions

As discussed in earlier chapters, the processes of the mind are quite simple. A vibration of energy forms a thought, the thought leads to a feeling, and the feeling creates an action. Sometimes people get lost in the intensity of thought, feeling, and emotion, never making it to the action stage. Thoughts and feelings can be like Velcro and it is difficult to break through, especially when experiencing an increase in stress. The intensity of the thoughts and feelings are so strong that some people cannot stop focusing on this mental "noise." In addition, their external world is not as interesting as their internal world. Awareness is the answer to this tendency. Practicing nondirective meditation, mindfulness techniques, and having increased body awareness can bring an experience of what is happening right now that naturally manifests as action. These practices provide the needed separation between awareness and the mind's creations. We will discuss these techniques in more detail in Chapter Sixteen.

Reason 3 - Unable to Drop the Why

I have worked with many people who come to therapy asking, "Why can't I change?" The WHY becomes more important than the change itself. This is a common area in which we get in our own way. "Why" is overrated; it is only helpful if there is something that happened in the past that a person cannot let go of because of a lack of understanding. Psychotherapy can help in situations like this, but most of the time after processing an issue enough times, it is best to drop the why. For example, I know someone who did not have a very good relationship with both his parents. He felt mistreated and emotionally abused. Now that he is middle-aged with a successful marriage and career, he has the opportunity to have less contact with his parents, which was the clinical recommendation. However, he answers every phone call, visits them regularly and complains how they still criticize him after all these years. Instead of changing his behavior, he continues to ask why they treat him badly. It's time to drop that question. Asking "why" delays action and is a manifestation of resistance. Instead, it would be beneficial to switch the question to "why not?"

Reason 4 - False Identification

This is a subtle but serious barrier to change. A person is identified with how they are and have fear of change, even if how they are is not working. This is common in the addiction field. The ego, once again, is the culprit. The ego tells the person he or she is overweight, for example, and the person perceives themselves as an overweight person. They are used to emotional eating, they are comfortable in the oversized clothes, and they are familiar with *wanting* to be thinner more than actually being thinner. Sometimes they have an unconscious wish to stay overweight because they are used to how the world treats them as an overweight person. There is safety in familiarity. Familiarity is the greatest barrier to change and that familiar feeling is based on the inaccurate identification. We are not what we think and feel about ourselves. These are just temporary descriptions. Our future is a field of many possibilities and infinite potentiality. Our true identity is the inner awareness observing everything else.

Reason 5 - Ignoring the Problem

Ignoring is one of the three tendencies of the mind mentioned in Chapter Five (grasping, resisting, and ignoring). If an unhealthy behavior or habit is ignored, there is no hope for change unless a big event intervenes. When a person acknowledges something they ignore and takes responsibility for it, an interesting tendency happens. Things often change by themselves when they are acknowledged. An example of this is my husband's ability to quit smoking. He did not choose a quit date. He did not slowly decrease the cigarettes he smoked each day. He did not use any smoking cessation props or a support group. He had the intention of living without smoking. He practiced LSF Meditation and allowed himself to do what he naturally felt like doing each day. His smoking naturally decreased on its own until one day he realized he had not had a cigarette in months. He never returned to smoking. The effort was in the intention, not the behavior. It's all about awareness, letting go of the struggle, and getting out of your own way, which leads to spontaneous reconfiguration.

Reason 6 - Secondary Gains

Some people unconsciously or consciously choose not to make a change because of the secondary gains of staying the same. Maybe people in the person's life care for them more or protect them without question, due to the way they are. If a change occurs, the person may fear the loss of this attention, unconditional nurturance, or even financial assistance. Relationships are immensely affected by this. There are countless examples of one partner changing their habits and their spouse not liking the change. Relationships often cannot sustain changes unless the communication is honest and open, trust and loyalty are intact, and the basis for the relationship is solid. As a person changes, they cannot expect unconditional support and acceptance from others.

If any of these reasons resonate with your situation, contemplate and process this insight. It is important not to feel bad about this realization, but to learn and grow from it. If change is what you seek, know the barriers keeping you from moving forward and readjust your path. Here are five suggestions to help you succeed with your intentions for change:

1. **Chain reaction change.** It is more difficult to change one area of your life than it is to change several areas at once. There is a momentum that provides a natural push when an action occurs. That momentum can increase when it is supported in several areas. If you want to start exercising again, try adding a new recreational activity to your schedule, call an old friend you haven't spoken to, and take new supplements or vitamins to help your strength and stamina. There is strength in numbers so increase the number of things you can change in your life.

2. **Change for you, not for anyone else**. Most people would agree if you change habits for someone else it will not sustain. Also, if you decide to change for you, don't expect everyone to agree with you. Some may want you to stay as you are.

3. **Create a ritual.** Rituals are helpful because they bring the sacred into the potentially boring routines in life. For example, if you decide to meditate once per day and just sit in any seat for twenty minutes, following your breath, and then go about your day, you most likely will stop meditating. However, if you have a special place to meditate, wear a special outfit, burn incense and light a candle, it feels very special. Actions that you perceive as special and sacred,

you will most likely look forward to doing regularly. Create a ritual around whatever you want to change.

4. **Delayed gratification.** When trying to decrease an unhealthy habit that you enjoy, pleasure is the driving force. It is difficult to succeed well at fighting pleasure, especially when you feel stressed because you want pleasure even more. There is nothing wrong with that; it is human nature. The best strategy is to delay the gratification. Some examples: "I don't have to have a cigarette right now, I can wait until later," "I will wait twenty minutes before getting seconds," "I will put this money in a drawer to buy a scratch-off later instead of going right now." The need for pleasure starts in the mind so interrupting the momentum is the key.

5. **Form a new habit.** It has been said that new habits and behaviors become solidified when practiced for twenty-one days straight. This is why many rehabilitation programs are 21-day commitments. Whatever behavior you want to implement, or habit you want to change, do it every day. I have found when I tell myself I will exercise at the gym three times per week, I miss the mark often. It dwindles to once per week. But if I plan on going to the gym every day, I actually stick to it better. If I miss a day or two due to not feeling well, it is still a lot more exercise than I was doing. Forming new habits is the best way to get out of your own way.

LSF Takeaway #14

Change is inevitable. Everything changes, nothing is permanent. Just the experience of awareness is unchanging and constant. Everything is transitory. Knowing this fact can be liberating. It is essential to understanding and experiencing presence and mindful living. Choose from the five suggestions listed in this chapter to help get you started with the change you seek.

Remember, "Just Do It" isn't just a Nike slogan, it really works! Instead of thinking about the change you want — just do it.

CHAPTER 15

Emotional Deliberation

> *We dance round in a ring and suppose,*
> *But the Secret sits in the middle and knows.*
> — ROBERT FROST

n Chapter Fourteen we explored how we get in our own way of making changes. This chapter is going to take this tendency to the next level and "kick it up a notch" as the celebrity chef Emeril Lagasse would say. When learning how we get in our own way from the previous chapter, it was stated: "Our true identity is the inner awareness observing everything else." This perception is a key concept that will transform every aspect of life when it is understood and experienced.

When you dream at night, what sees your dream so you know what it was about when you wake up? It could not have been the mind, because it was busy having the dream. Your inner awareness saw the dream. This awareness is always present and never changing. It is aware of your mind as you go about your day. It watches your thoughts, feelings, and actions that take place all day long. It is the witness of your life and the only part of you that is not transitory and impermanent. Everything comes and goes except for this awareness.

Awareness is always calm. It is grounded, centered, stable, and connected to everything. Awareness feels like love, joy, and trust. It can be accessed anytime when you practice a technique that allows you to experience this awareness, which we will learn in Chapter Sixteen. Most people are unable to access awareness when they are not practicing a technique designed to experience it. The mind can take over so strongly, that the underlying awareness is blocked completely, much like mud can change the color of a river or lake, or dust can distort a mirror. When we are struggling with an issue, conflict, or frustration, it is especially difficult to access awareness.

Emotional Deliberation is a technique designed to "take the wind out of the sails" of the mind that gets in the way of experiencing the ever-present awareness. When you are ambivalent or struggling with a challenging issue, the usual reaction is to problem solve it as soon as possible so the discomfort will be lifted. Emotional Deliberation is not about problem-solving, nor is it about trying to find a compromise. It is designed to take the steam out of the problem through exploring all sides of it without judgment. When you try and solve a dilemma you are struggling with, you inject more energy and strength into that problem. The problem pits you against yourself. When you simply explore all sides of a situation, it diffuses the struggle. Contemplating all sides of the issue brings awareness into the dilemma which will infuse the qualities of awareness into your thoughts, feelings, and actions.

How does Emotional Deliberation work? The definition for deliberation is "long and careful consideration or discussion." It involves advocating for different sides. That is what you will be doing through this technique by advocating and honoring all perspectives instead of using your mind to choose the *right* answer or deciding what you *should* do.

The Emotional Deliberation Technique

1. Choose an issue, dilemma or conflict that is creating frustration, ambivalence, or struggle.
2. Begin by identifying the two opposite sides to the issue: the polarization. These are the two opposite ways of perceiving the situation: "Either I do this or I do that."
3. Give the perspectives form by addressing each side of the struggle, asking questions, and defending each side's position. This can be

done by writing to each side or actually talking out loud to each side: the "empty chair" technique, which will be described in the case study that follows. Use the word "you" not "I" when addressing each side. Playing both parts validates and honors each side.

4. Go deeper and explore the hopes and fears of each side.
5. Examine the mental tendencies to grasp, resist, or ignore aspects of each side.
6. Through this exploration notice if a new side emerges: the third option. Fully contemplate this additional perspective.
7. Honor all perspectives without judgment. There is no right or wrong answer.

Become accepting of the uncertainty and allow awareness to sit with your ambivalence. Remember, awareness feels like love, joy, and trust. You are loving all sides of yourself. This honoring and cherishing will cultivate joy and happiness through the validation and you will trust that the universe, God, nature, or whatever form of spirituality works for you, will reveal the best action through tapping into awareness. Your inner awareness feels secure and will allow you to sit with uncertainty.

Case Study

A client we will call Sue tried the Emotional Deliberation Technique in a recent workshop my husband and I led. Her dilemma was whether to continue her extremely busy schedule of working full time, taking online courses toward her Master's Degree, raising two daughters, six and nine years old, and enjoying her relationship with her significant other or begin carving out more time for herself to rest, enjoy her hobbies and interests, and have extra downtime.

She first addressed the side of her that is extremely busy, talking to that side out loud by directing her comments to an empty chair. She confronted this busy side by stating, "You are doing too much ... you think you are Wonder Woman ... you can't keep going on like this ... you are neglecting your children and boyfriend." She continued in this way until she said everything she could think of to the busy part of her, speaking as if this was a separate person. Then, she switched chairs and spoke to the part of her that wants to relax more stating, "You are a slacker ... you are just trying to take the easy way out because it's so hard ... what would other people think about you if you don't give 100% to your goals."

The next step was for Sue to discuss her hopes and fears of living in this busy way. She sat in the other chair and defended this side of her. Her hope is that she will accomplish her educational goals, be able to get a better, higher paying job, and have more time and money for her family when she is done. Other people would be proud of her accomplishments and she will feel good about herself. The fear is that she will miss out on her daughters growing up during important times in their lives, she will not give her boyfriend enough attention which may hurt their relationship, and her health may suffer. She then sat in the other chair and reviewed the hopes and fears of living her life in a more relaxed way. Her hope is that she will enjoy her life more now, not missing out on anything. She will get more rest, have time to exercise and eat more healthfully. She can enjoy more fun activities, have time to recreate, and maybe start playing her guitar again. Her fear is that she will never finish her degree and will always feel like she lost her opportunity.

She then looked at her mental tendencies of grasping, resisting, and ignoring. Her contemplation of this revealed she is attached to accomplishment and achievement but is ignoring her basic needs and her health. She had an emotional reaction to this, with some tearfulness. This is when the "third door" appeared, as discussed in the First Chapter. She realized she is making decisions based on her ideas instead of the reality of her situation. That was all that needed to be done. Her final decision will be up to her, but it will be a well thought out decision.

This technique allows inner awareness to enter the conflict because it was her awareness that witnessed the different sides of Sue. As long as she perceived the situation as "I want this," or "I want that," she was identifying with the mind that was creating the dilemma. The only way around this conundrum is to identify with the awareness.

The first rule to remember when practicing this technique is to take full responsibility for your thoughts, feelings, and actions. This can be difficult because it requires raw vulnerability and utmost honesty. For some, this is a challenge, but it is necessary to fully examine a stressful dilemma.

I worked with a client who came from a family that reinforced secretive behavior. She was raised this way and kept secrets from family members, friends, and coworkers. She only shared these secrets in therapy sessions. The problem with this strategy was she experienced constant anxiety and worry that someone would find out the truth. Living with hidden secrets, lies, and dishonesty will never solve conflicts and frustrations.

The second element of this technique is going beyond preconceived ideas or beliefs of right and wrong, praise and blame, or judgment of any kind. It is the essence of nonjudgmental awareness, which is a common definition of mindfulness. Hope and fear are actually destructive forces that interfere with accessing the awareness that exists within and without.

Hope and fear come from feeling that we lack something;
they come from a sense of poverty. We can't simply relax
with ourselves. We hold on to hope, and hope robs
us of the present moment. We feel that someone else knows
what's going on, but that there's something missing
in us, and therefore something is lacking
in our world.
Rather than letting our negativity get the better of us, we
could acknowledge that right now we feel like a piece of shit
and not be squeamish about taking a good look. That's the
compassionate thing to do. That's the brave thing to do.
We can't just jump over ourselves as if we were not there.
It's better to take a straight look at all our hopes and fears.
Then some kind of confidence in our basic sanity arises.
— PEMA CHÖDRON
FROM THE BOOK "WHEN THINGS FALL APART:
HEART ADVICE FOR DIFFICULT TIMES"

How do you know if you are making a decision from this awareness and not the mind? This is easier than you think. Only the mind thinks and feels the negative states you experience, not awareness. Take the "I" out of how you perceive difficulties and the perspective changes. For example, instead of thinking, "I am depressed" say to yourself, "Mind is depressed." It is not you, it is your mind. You are not your mind. "Mind is angry," "mind feels pain," not you. With addictions, the mind wants a drink, not "I want a drink."

Inner awareness has no depression, no anger, no pain, no cravings. The awareness is content, happy, and fulfilled. You are awareness, not the mind. Seeing this separation is extremely important to answer the age-old question: "Who Am I?" The answer to this question is *awareness*, and connecting with who you really are is all you have to do to make decisions, progress in life, and enjoy fulfillment in all areas.

LSF Takeaway #15

The Emotional Deliberation Technique will help you experience your inner awareness: the place inside you where everything in your moment by moment experience begins. Accessing awareness is more useful and important than finding a solution right away. Becoming aware of awareness will bring new perspectives into the equation. This awareness reveals that what your mind thinks is often inaccurate or distorted because it is based on the ego or past impressions. It is only one side of the story. Conflicts and challenges are often not the way you think they are. Conflicts are created by the mind, not you. You are not your mind. You are your awareness.

Choose a conflict to try the Emotional Deliberation Technique with. Follow the step-by-step instructions in this chapter. Write down the process and your insights in your journal.

CHAPTER 16

The Best Meditation Technique You Can Do

Although this title is a bold statement, I can say with complete certainty from my knowledge and experience, that the method of meditation outlined in this chapter is the best technique to lower stress. What makes a meditation technique "the best?" It is simple, easy, and understandable; it does not cost much money; it doesn't take long to practice each day, and it's efficient. It brings tangible, sustainable results and anyone can practice it. It's a technique you can comfortably fit into your daily schedule to provide much needed "me-time." It's a technique that gives you an effective tool to change your relationship with stressful experiences head-on instead of providing a pleasurable escape that temporarily distracts you from the stressful feelings.

Meditation has been around a long time and many types of meditation exist. There are different goals for different forms of meditation. The definition of meditation is also varied, depending on where you look. The type of meditation I recommend, to gain the insight and experiences discussed throughout this book, is LSF Nondirective Mindfulness Meditation.

Here are Ten Truisms about LSF Meditation:

1. It does not require concentration on one fixed object, a thought, or the breath.
2. It does not require anything to believe because it is based on an experience and not a thought or idea.

3. It is a technique, not a religious practice.
4. It is not in conflict with any religion; in fact, it enhances people's religious practices.
5. The technique is extremely simple and easy.
6. You do not have to clear your mind or stop yourself from thinking.
7. It can be practiced anywhere, anytime.
8. It requires 15-20 minutes per day — that's it.
9. It will direct you to your inner awareness and help you experience this awareness even when not meditating.
10. It dissolves stress spontaneously.

The only discipline needed for the practice is to just do it every day. The rest is effortless. The practice of nondirective meditation is a state of alert awareness. You sit completely aware of everything you are experiencing, but you do not engage with any of it. You are part of your experience and you are witnessing your experience simultaneously.

The technique requires just you, without the need for anything additional, such as music, nature sounds, a completely silent space, or a candle to focus on. The point of the technique is to experience things as they are, without interfering. This means you could meditate in your home, your car, in a park, on break at your office, in a doctor's office waiting room, or even in the middle of a noisy city.

Only through nondirective meditation can you truly notice what *is*, without interfering with the experience. You are not interacting with anything, which allows you to be completely aware of how your breathing, physical body, thoughts, and feelings operate. Only through nondirective sitting meditation can you truly do nothing and just observe everything. You become the greatest scientist or investigator of your own body and mind. This kind of raw awareness allows you to know yourself inside and out. The best part is that this awareness, which requires doing nothing but observing, creates change. You cannot change anything if you are unaware of what is happening internally and externally.

It is very important to realize the distinction between meditation and contemplation. Many people mistake meditation for contemplation. In non-directive meditation, the practitioner is aware of thoughts and feelings as they arise and pass. If the meditator naturally starts thinking about a thought, he or she allows themselves to think but continues to stay aware of everything in perceptual experience. With contemplation, a person purposely chooses a specific idea to focus on. This is usually a spiritual passage, a religious figure, an inspirational quote, or a visual experience. Although there is merit to this practice, the goal and result are not the same as nondirective meditation. Because the person is inserting something into their moment, they are not truly experiencing the moment as it is. The practice of experiencing the present moment — mindfulness — is not occurring with contemplation. These are two completely different practices.

True mindfulness is nondirective meditation. Your attention is placed on the constantly changing experiences of the moment to moment awareness. The only thing that does not change is your awareness itself. During LSF Meditation practice, one does not engage with anything but is aware of everything. This is the training ground for the tasks and activities of the day. After the meditation practice finishes, the state of mindfulness continues spontaneously, and it becomes easier to stay fully present, responding to situations instead of reacting to them and living with alert calmness. Over time, this becomes the natural state the meditator enjoys on a daily basis. This is living stress-free!

Here are three important points to remember before embarking on your meditation journey.

1. **Nondirective meditation is a goal-less practice.** If you sit with the goal to feel more relaxed, you are defeating the purpose. The point is to observe moment to moment experiences. You may get relaxed from it, or you may not. It does not matter either way. The only goal is to be aware of the moment, continuously.

2. **There is no such thing as a good meditation or a bad meditation.** Good and bad are just comparisons and judgments created

by the mind and the ego. These qualifiers have nothing to do with the point of meditation. When you sit and do nothing but observe your experience, your mental, emotional, and physical stress becomes more obvious and you may feel the effects of this. The mind wants to interpret this as a "bad thing." Just see the mind for what it is: a bubble machine churning out thoughts based on your past, as we learned in Chapter Three. LSF Meditation teaches us to stop paying so much attention to our habitual thoughts as if they are relevant.

3. **Every meditation is different; have no expectations.** Just like the weather is slightly different each day, so is the practice of moment to moment awareness. If life wasn't always evolving and changing, it would certainly get quite boring. Cultivate curiosity and enjoy riding the wave of the present moment no matter where it takes you.

Are you ready to learn? Here's a quick review:

- The goal is not to concentrate on one object such as the breath, a thought, a body part, or a sound.
- The goal is not to stop thinking or block out any thoughts, feelings or sounds.
- The goal is not relaxation; it is awareness.
- The best strategy to adopt is "add, don't subtract": If you get drawn into focusing on part of your experience as you sit, add more of what is happening at that moment; include everything you are noticing or aware or without interacting with it.

The Living Stress Free® Meditation Technique

- Sit in a comfortable, upright, alert position.
- Rest your hands on your thighs or in your lap.
- Keep your eyes open and just gaze downward, not focusing on anything specific. If this is uncomfortable, close your eyes at first,

but eventually try to keep them open. Keeping all senses open is an important part of the practice.

- As you breathe, notice the feeling of the air going in and out of your body, either at the level of your nostrils or upper lip. Don't try and change your breathing; just feel the sensation of the breath as it occurs naturally.
- Notice the feeling of your body as you sit. This includes all parts of your body. You can do a body scan if you'd like, intentionally bringing awareness from your feet all the way to the top of your head. Be aware of all bodily feelings and sensations.
- Be aware of sounds in your environment; notice sounds coming and going.
- Be aware of thoughts and feelings coming and going.
- Sit for 15-20 minutes remaining aware of your breath, physical sensations, sounds, smells, tastes, thoughts, emotions, and what you see in your environment. This is an all-inclusive practice; do not exclude anything that occurs.
- If you find yourself thinking about a thought, let yourself think. Just include the breath, body, and sounds while you think.
- Do not try and control anything; do not struggle with anything. Just be in the moment as it unfolds.

You will realize when you follow the technique as stated above, mindfulness is naturally occurring. All of your senses are open and aware. You hear sounds, you see what's in front of you, you smell and taste if applicable, and you are acutely aware of your sense of touch by feeling your body sitting. As discussed in earlier chapters, the mind is seen as a sixth sense and you are aware of the mind creating thoughts as this occurs. It is easy to think about these thoughts at first because that is a habitual pattern. But adding the other parts of your experience that are beyond the mind, such as breath and sounds, helps the tendency to think have less importance. Over time you will just watch the thoughts come and go as you sit. It is a fascinating experience.

Why is this the best meditation technique you can do? I have been practicing different meditation techniques since 1992. I did not learn from a YouTube video, a blog, or an EAP seminar. I studied for 25 years under authentic meditation masters in the yogic and Buddhist traditions, where meditation originally came from. The commonalities between the different meditation techniques, as well as the results, were similar. However, nondirective meditation seemed to be the simplest, easiest method for anyone to reach the same state that other techniques brought me to. It also is completely secular, which prevents anyone from resisting it for religious reasons.

When teaching this method to clients, the main feedback I've received is how they love the fact they did not have to stop their thoughts or thinking processes; they were not told to clear their mind. This lack of struggle was an unexpected benefit and gratefully appreciated. Many people with panic attacks, anxiety, and depression have shared how they experienced great relief from these mental states and symptoms due to their daily meditation practice.

Another level of significance that pertains to anyone practicing LSF Meditation, is the effect of the practice on living life with ease. How you sit becomes how you live. Other meditation techniques, especially the ones requiring any kind of concentration, are effective during the time a person meditates but the results are rarely sustained. A person cannot go through the day focusing on their breath. This is not possible unless you live in a monastery or ashram. You cannot do work responsibilities while focusing on a particular mantra constantly or reciting an inspirational phrase. Life inevitably interferes. However, the act of just sitting without interfering with the moment, and learning how to be attentive, alert, and open to the moment, allowing the moment to unfold, is a perfect way to live life 24/7. Only this meditation method offers that. Life spontaneously becomes like meditation. The meditator learns how to accept with openness, tolerate discomfort, and maintain awareness of the transitory essence of everything. No matter how difficult it gets managing life's stressors, the meditator knows it will pass. This wisdom is immeasurable. LSF Meditation allows for this to occur without trying: it is completely natural and spontaneous. This is why I feel confident in stating it is the best meditation technique you can do.

The one caveat in learning LSF Meditation from this book is that you will not get the full benefit of the practice without the guidance of a Certified Living Stress Free Meditation instructor to offer a personal explanation, troubleshooting, and support. The instructions are a wonderful foundation and can easily get you started, but I strongly recommend visiting livingstressfree.org for more direction on how to work with a teacher through eMeditation.

LSF Takeaway #16

Nondirective meditation is the easiest method to begin imbibing, experiencing, understanding, and incorporating all of the suggestions discussed throughout each chapter in this book. If you are truly inspired and motivated to live a stress-free life, meditation is necessary. I recommend a consistent daily practice that becomes as natural to you as brushing your teeth each day. Begin by practicing LSF Nondirective Mindfulness Meditation each day for a designated period of time. You can start with ten minutes and work yourself up to twenty. Follow the instructions exactly as they are described in this chapter. The directions are meant to be followed accurately, without altering any of the steps. It helps to choose a time of day that works well for you. Create a ritual to make it your special time to just take care of you. Continue to practice every day, to lower your stress and live a healthier, happier life. Keep a meditation journal and write down your insights from your practice. You will learn more about yourself from this practice than most anything else you will ever do.

CHAPTER 17

Music Therapy, Mindfulness, and Healing

Music gives a soul to the universe, wings to the mind,
flight to the imagination and life to everything
— PLATO

According to the definition from the American Music Therapy Association, "Music therapy is the clinical and evidence-based use of music interventions to accomplish individualized goals within a therapeutic relationship by a credentialed professional who has completed an approved music therapy program. Music therapy is an established health profession in which music is used within a therapeutic relationship to address physical, emotional, cognitive, and social needs of individuals."

I have worked as a board-certified music therapist since 1988. Although music therapists work with all types of individuals with disabilities, the scope of my practice for my entire career has been the adult psychiatric population. For thirty years I have seen the benefit of using music and sound to change thoughts, emotions, and behaviors in people who suffer from imbalances due to mental illness. Music is definitely a change agent. It has a physiological effect on the recipient that reaches more than just the person's thoughts and feelings; music is a whole body experience.

Soon after becoming a music therapist, I began my journey toward personal and spiritual development through learning meditation and yoga in 1992. Through studying and practicing ancient techniques from the yogic and Buddhist traditions, I became acutely aware of that which is beyond the mind; the one thing that is always present and never changing. There are many names for this place depending on the tradition, such as the Self, the Witness, Buddha Nature, Atman, and Brahman. All refer to a state of awareness that is omnipresent, alert, calm, blissful, and loving in how it feels to the one experiencing it. This state can be experienced through the ancient practices of meditation and yoga, as well as through Kirtan chanting and sound techniques based on Vedic India's spiritual music-sound traditions.

Through the years it began to occur to me there is a strong commonality and integration between accessing core awareness and the experience of feeling music-sound vibrations. In fact, several traditional yogic and Buddhist techniques that I've practiced included music, such as chanting, nada yoga, and drumming. Experiencing these practices brought me to the state of core awareness. The spiritual music-sound traditions of many indigenous peoples include this goal of experiencing core awareness — going beyond the mind. As a music therapist, it intrigued me to find a way to share this knowledge in my work.

I integrated traditional mindfulness meditation and yogic practices using sound and music into my sessions with the mental health clients I served, with excellent results. Not only did their symptoms of depression, anxiety, obsessive thought patterns, mental confusion, and even panic attacks decrease, some of them experienced their core awareness, by their report. There was an opportunity for more than just improvement, they began to heal.

Music therapy has the potential to help everyone. You do not need a diagnosis to receive the benefits. The healing effects of sound, when used to connect with core awareness, is a universal practice based on nature and ancient wisdom, not limited to a specific population of people. It's my intention to bridge the traditional definition of music therapy to the general public.

Music was my refuge. I could crawl into the space
between the notes and curl my back to loneliness.
— MAYA ANGELOU

How can you use music-sound therapy for stress-free living? Here are four basic practices you can begin to experiment with to eradicate the effects of stress from your daily experience of life. Each practice is a mindfulness technique as well.

Music Baths

Stress management classes and self-help blogs reinforce the helpfulness of listening to music for relaxation and distraction during stressful times. However, rarely do I hear people explain *how* to listen to music as a stress reduction and stress prevention tool. Here are three golden rules for using music to reduce and prevent stress by taking music baths, no water necessary.

The first rule is to refrain from choosing music with lyrics unless they are in a language you are unfamiliar with. Lyrics will activate your thinking processes and distract you from the here and now. The words to songs can fascinate you, give you something to contemplate, or remind you of times in the past when a situation occurred. The simple act of listening to music has now turned into a walk down memory lane or become a springboard for internal dialogue. Choose instrumental music, the less familiar the better, so the past impressions of your mind do not sabotage your experience.

The second rule is to stop yourself from treating the music as secondary while you do something else. If you are using music listening therapeutically, just listen to the music without doing anything else. Background music is perfectly fine for the purpose of enhancing your tasks, such as listening to music while working out at the gym, but it is not going to give you the full stress decreasing ability it is capable of if combined with other activities.

The third rule is to carve out a workable period of time to practice this technique. If you listen to music while thinking about all the other things you have to do, forget it! It will only cause you more stress. Choose a time of day that lends itself to winding down and set a timer. Have the intention to use that period of time just for you to help lower your stress level through music listening. It's your "me time."

How to enjoy a Music Bath:

- Select the recorded music you want to listen to, using any format that would not include commercials.
- Sit or lay down in any comfortable place where you won't be disturbed, such as your favorite chair, your bed, or any place where you are close to your music source (this is not a traditional bath in water).
- Set a timer or choose music that is timed for a certain length.
- Close your eyes and listen to the music; mindfully and completely listen to the music you are hearing, undisturbed.
- Listen to what instruments you hear and how the dynamics shift (how soft or loud the music becomes). Notice tempo changes, silences, the mood you are feeling from the music, and where the melody takes you.
- Notice your breathing patterns and your body sensations while you listen. Be aware of your breathing slowing down or your muscles relaxing more. Experience any changes in your heart rate or overall posture.
- Pay attention to how bathing your mind and body in the music shifts your focus from the transient stress of the day to your core awareness, helping you feel grounded, centered, and calm.

The Iso-Principle

"Iso-principle is a technique by which music is matched with the mood of a client, then gradually altered to affect the desired mood state. This technique can also be used to affect physiological responses such as heart rate and blood pressure" (Davis, Gfeller, & Thaut, 2008). The term iso-principle originated in 1948, as a concept and method of intervention in the context of mood management (Altshulter, 1948) and is specific to music therapy. The basic premise is this: match the music you play or listen to with the current way you are feeling. The music will resonate with your body-mind-spirit which results in feeling validated and supported. Next, change the music to a style that demonstrates how you would like to feel. Since music has such a powerful physiological effect, there is a strong likelihood your mood will change to the desired feeling state through the principle of entrainment. It is a highly effective mood management tool.

The caveat to this technique is how individualized it is. What one person finds to be an angry sounding piece of music, another person may find relaxing. Music that brings you happiness may make another person terribly annoyed. E. A. Bucchianeri's famous quote, "Art is in the eye of the beholder, and everyone will have their own interpretation," is a perfect example of this truism. Music is in the ear of the beholder and only they can say what effect it has on them.

I worked with a client who struggled with a lot of anger. He excessively drank alcohol to self-medicate and take the edge off his anger. In an effort to find healthier ways to decrease his anger, we created a mood management playlist to help shift his mood. We chose four angry-sounding songs he was familiar with, that resonated with his frustration. After uploading them onto his playlist, we chose two neutral songs: music he liked but songs that were not agitating. To finish the playlist, he chose four more songs that were calming. We decided not to choose "happy party music" type selections because they might increase his desire to drink alcohol. The relaxing music helped him rest and "chill-out." He listened to his playlist on weekends, when he had the most difficulty with his urges to drink, and found it helped tremendously.

How to use the Iso-Principle:

- Decide what emotional state you have a tendency to struggle with, causing stress reactions. For example, some people struggle with anger, others sadness. Any emotion that is difficult for you is applicable.
- Create a customized playlist: find music that matches the emotional state you struggle with and put three or four selections on a playlist or CD compilation.

- Next, select one or two musical selections or songs that are less intense, more neutral, and add these to the playlist.
- Finally, finish the playlist with three or four songs that match how you want to feel.
- The entire playlist or CD should be approximately thirty minutes long.
- Listen to it whenever you want to change your mood.
- If you play an instrument you can use this same process by creating your own live performance to shift your mood.

Vocal Toning

Toning is the process of sustained vocalizing of a single vowel sound for therapeutic benefit. There are no melodies, rhythms, or words; there is just the vibration of the sound. Through vocal toning, the participant will experience the sound and its impact on specific parts of the body. Our bodies are designed to feel vibrations. Our skeletal framework is the perfect resonating chamber for vibrations to reverberate. Depending on the vowel sound chosen, a vibration will be felt in a certain area of the body that can help loosen and release the stress that may be locked in that area. Toning provides a massage from the inside.

I have practiced toning on different occasions while driving to an anxiety-provoking meeting, an interview, and an audition. I vocalized the sound "ahh" for as long as I could sustain it, for 5-6 rounds. I felt the vibration in my throat area, the back of my neck, and my chest. This began to loosen and open up these areas, releasing the tension. In addition, sustaining the sound as long as possible expelled most of the air in my lungs with the extended exhalation. This activated the parasympathetic nervous system which helped my body release toxins and induced a relaxation response.

Toning is accessible to everyone, with no prerequisites of vocal ability or training. It is not singing — it is sounding. Toning allows you to experience the effects of sound vibration on your physical, mental, emotional, and spiritual well-being. In my work with clients, toning has been particularly helpful for folks who have difficulty breathing properly due to anxiety. If exhaling is difficult, tension is often the cause. By vocalizing a sound, exhalation is occurring but the client is not focused on it. The sound vibration will be the focus. Psychologically, as well as physically, the tension will be released.

Here are a few examples of vowel sounds that can be used and where one might feel the vibration:

UU (as in who) - the base of the spine: very grounding and calming
OH (as in toe) - solar plexus: stabilizing and quieting the mind
AH (as in car) - heart area: centering and expanding
AY (as in pray) - neck and throat: increasing confidence
EE (as in knee) - head: energizing
MM (humming) - whole body balancing

When I first introduced toning to my clients, some were skeptical. A certain level of self-consciousness arises and past impressions of new age practitioners leading free-spirited seekers in ecstatic chanting come to mind. However, once my clients let go of their judgments and tried the toning practice, many of them were pleasantly surprised, if not hooked on it! It's the same message that is the undercurrent of this entire book: have beginner's mind, be fully present, and stay curious. Do not let your past impressions interfere with your present reality.

How to use Vocal Toning:

- Find a place you will feel comfortable toning, without disturbing others.
- Start with a hum, the MM sound, and sustain it as long as you can.
- Breathe in and repeat for approximately four to six rounds, but do not get too focused on counting.
- Feel your body and notice where the vibration is occurring; listen to the sound you are creating.

- After experiencing the humming, try different vowel sounds in the same way and see how they feel in the body.
- The entire practice only needs to be 5-10 minutes.
- After you're finished, it helps to sit in silence and feel your breath and your body, noticing any changes in your thoughts and emotions. Toning is an excellent way to practice mindfulness.

A good groove releases adrenaline in your body.
You feel uplifted, you feel centered, you feel calm,
you feel powerful. You feel that energy.
That's what good drumming is all about.
— MICKEY HART

Drumming

If anyone ever told you that you have no musical ability or you have no rhythm, he or she misinformed you. Before you were born you heard your mother's heartbeat. Your body right now has its own rhythm as a result of your pulse, metabolism, breathing patterns, inner vibrations, and of course the main drum inside — your heartbeat. You can feel the rhythm.

Drumming is the original expression of music since the beginning of time and its presence exists in every culture around the world. The influence of drumming on the mind and body manifests on a kinesthetic level, tapping into core awareness, going beyond the thinking mind. The therapeutic use of drumming harnesses the natural power of rhythm to shift awareness for the purpose of healing. Drumming releases suppressed emotions, loosens inhibitions, allows for creative expression and cultivates a feeling of universality when practiced with others. As discussed in Chapter Eleven, fear exists whenever there is a feeling of separation. The prevalence of an "us-and-them" mentality has been creating an epidemic of fear and anxiety throughout society as a whole. The feeling of connection that drumming provides is the perfect antidote to the perception of separation that exists.

I'd like to dispel some misconceptions about drumming. When I started incorporating the use of drumming in my music therapy practice, some of the clients I worked with were almost paralyzed with fear about touching a drum. There is this underlying past impression of insecurity about doing the wrong thing that many people struggle with. However, you don't have to play like Buddy Rich to use a drum therapeutically. If you have ever tapped your toe to music, moved your fingers or hands to a song while driving, or danced, you can play the drum just fine. The mind loves to raise the bar of aptitude and demand perfection. Be aware of this tendency and let it go. Even when these self-critical thoughts arise while playing, let them go.

Another misconception is the belief you need a leader to follow. This lack of trust in yourself is most likely in other areas of life as well. Unlock your creativity. It's there, it just needs expression. Explore how to create sound and play with the silence. Nobody is judging you and there is no audience to please. There is no right or wrong in your expression. It can be a liberating experience to play your feelings on a drum to release them. There is nothing worse for your stress level than allowing difficult feelings to stay locked inside with no way to express or process them. Give your feelings a voice through sound. It has an amazing healing potential that will help reduce your stress.

How to use Drumming:

You will need a drum. Drums are easy to find at all price ranges. You can even adapt something already in your household to use as a drum, such as a large plastic container, bucket, or old suitcase. My favorite drums to use for therapeutic purposes are djembes and frame drums.

- Drumming for stress relief: Find a video or play a recording of any type of music that has a strong beat and play along. Experience the rhythm as a mindfulness practice and listen with your whole body. Do not use the drumming as a time to think. Drumming is an experience; the less thinking the better. Try to practice drumming for at least ten minutes, preferably twenty. The longer you play the more you get in "the zone" and your thinking mind will quiet down.

- Drumming to express feelings: When you have strong feelings about something stressful that happened, play your feelings on the drum. If the feeling was set to music, what would it sound like? Nobody is critiquing this practice, it is just for you. Giving emotions form, outside of yourself, is a very helpful way to work through issues.
- Drum circles: If you have the option of trying a drum circle in your area, go for it! It can be a wonderful way to have fun and get rid of the stress.

These four music therapy practices are a springboard for experiencing how music and sound can create change on a physical, mental, emotional, and spiritual level. To fully reap the benefits of music therapy, I recommend working with a credentialed music therapist. There are certain nuances and adjustments to the use of music for therapeutic purposes that are individualized and specific to your physiology. Board-certified music therapists have the knowledge and training to help you get the best results from your practice.

A man should hear a little music, read a little poetry,
and see a fine picture every day of his life, in order
that worldly cares may not obliterate the sense of the
beautiful which God has implanted in the human soul.
— JOHANN WOLFGANG VON GOETHE

LSF Takeaway #17

Music is one of the easiest tools to access for lowering stress but often is dismissed or forgotten. The more stress a person feels, the less likely they will seek out healthy ways to decrease it. Use the techniques outlined in this chapter. Select either Music Baths, the Iso-Principle, Vocal Toning, or Drumming, and experiment with it this week. Better yet, try all four! At the very least, next time you are lost in thought or stuck in a feeling, play some music in your home, your car, or wherever you are. Allow the music to change your physiology.

CHAPTER 18
Balance in All Things: The Yantra

Not being tense but ready.
Not thinking but not dreaming.
Not being set but flexible.
Liberation from the uneasy sense of confinement.
It is being wholly and quietly alive, aware and
alert, ready for whatever may come.
— BRUCE LEE, *TAO OF JEET KUNE DO*

f I had to sum up the secret to living stress-free in two words, the first would be *awareness* and the second would be *balance*. Awareness is experienced through mindfulness practices and the suggestions throughout this book. Balance is the spontaneous result of consistent awareness practice.

The intent to achieve balance exists everywhere. All of creation is polarized and the pairs of opposites are forever seeking balance. Ancient yogic philosophy describes the beginning of existence in this way: There is one universal all-encompassing energy that is existence itself. There is only this energy; nothing else exists. This energy is pure love, pure light, pure being, divinity itself. At some point, this energy wanted to experience itself. The only way to experience itself was to become something separate from itself. This was the beginning of the creation of form, substance, and life as we know it. As the universal divine energy took form, it did so through becoming its opposite: polarization. To illustrate this point, you know what cold feels like because it's the opposite of hot. You understand pain because you have experienced pleasure. The way to know something is to compare it to its opposite. In the same way, the universal energy could only know itself through splitting itself into subject and object. All of universal existence is made from the same divine energy wanting to know itself. It knows itself through separation from itself. The irony is that knowing your opposite is only knowing part of the picture. The universal energy exists infinitely everywhere. It is beyond the pairs of opposites. This is where balance comes in. By finding your balance you can experience what is beyond the pairs of opposites. You will avoid the extremes and live in "the middle way" as Buddha taught.

To help you go beyond the pairs of opposites in your own life, there is a tool that assists in conceptualizing and making a concrete plan toward the experience of balance as a way of life. This tool is called the Living Stress Free Yantra. Yantra is the Sanskrit word for "instrument." It comes from the root "yam" which means supporting, checking, or holding the essence of an object or concept. The syllable "tra" comes from "trana" or liberation from bondage. Yantras can represent symbols, processes, or anything that has structure and organization. Yantras are visual tools that serve as centering devices. It is common for yantras to be symbols or geometric figures used as visualization techniques to balance the mind.

The Living Stress Free Yantra is an instrument used to organize and represent a basic conception of life in a holistic sense. It represents the eight universal aspects that exist in every person's experience of life in modern society. The purpose of using this yantra is to understand the importance of each aspect of your life, honor each area in some way on a regular basis, and experience balance. Inevitably, one of the main causes of stress is too much focus on one or two areas of the yantra with a tendency to ignore the rest, or decide "I will just get to that later." The problem is that *later* rarely comes. The best way to help decrease and prevent stress is through finding balance by honoring all eight areas in some way as often as possible, Balance results in more happiness, health, contentment, and fulfillment.

The Living Stress Free® Yantra

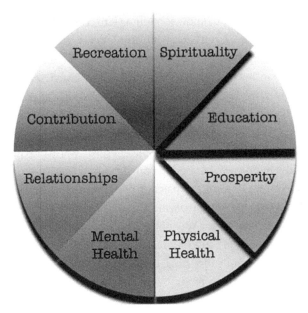

The LSF Yantra Eight Essential Areas

Relationships

Relationships encompass every type of relationship. This includes, but is not limited to, your spouse, significant other, children, friends, family, co-workers, acquaintances, professionals in your life, strangers at the grocery store, social media friends, and so on. It also includes your non-human relationships to pets, the trees in your yard, and your environment. Your reaction and communication with other beings have an impact on your stress level every day, for better or for worse. You have a direct and indirect exchange with other beings all the time, and how you choose to interact with the relationships around you affects your state of mind. Honoring relationships, in whatever form this takes, is as essential as breathing is to staying alive.

Relationship Suggestion: Pretend that every being you come across throughout your day was sent to you for a reason. What reason? To learn and to grow. Be open to the fact that others can improve your existence if you are aware of what they are offering you, whether it be in a helpful way or a challenging one. This will prevent aversion to others and help improve all relationships in your life.

Mental Health

Mental health includes the process of thinking, what you have a tendency to think about, the feelings that are created from thinking, and the behaviors that result. Do you have a clear mind or are you confused often? Do you get overwhelmed with thoughts? Do your thoughts tend to be positive or negative? Many people suffer from unhealthy emotional patterns, which lead to unhealthy behaviors. The source of this basic tendency is based on the thought patterns that start the process. First, there is a thought which leads to a feeling, resulting in a behavior. The secret to honoring your mind and having sound mental health is awareness of what your mind is doing.

Mental Health Suggestion: Each day, set a timer for two minutes and write down all the thoughts you have during that two minutes. Once the time is up, review your list. Are there themes or is it totally random? Did you notice the part of you that was able to observe the thoughts and write them down was separate from the part of you having the thoughts? That is important. You cannot change your unhealthy thought patterns unless you are aware of them from the part of you that is separate from the mind, which is *awareness*.

Spirituality

Spirituality refers to the deepest values and meanings by which people live. It is the inner path enabling a person to discover the essence of his or her being. Although religion is part of spirituality, it is not the totality of the concept. The best way to sum up the meaning of spirituality is the belief or experience that there is something greater than ourselves in the world that supports us, guides us, and gives meaning to our lives. This concept influences our values, our behaviors, and how we navigate our path in this world. If we don't honor this aspect of our lives in some way, life lacks meaning and purpose. Stress has a chance to grow as a person feels more isolated and empty. This significantly will affect balance in life and results in a lack of fulfillment, satisfaction, and contentment.

Spirituality Suggestion: Practice the art of surrender. Whenever the need or desire to control a situation is evident, let go. Surrender to the higher intelligence, the universal energy, the field of unknown possibilities, or the community at large, and see what happens. There is a greater intelligence beyond your mind. Trust and let go.

Recreation

Recreation is spending time in a way that refreshes one's body and mind. It is re-creating yourself! Recreation is active for the participant in a pleasurable, diverting manner. If you don't have to do it but you want to do it, if it's enjoyable and carefree — you are recreating! Your artistic interests, hobbies, leisure activities, downtime, and participation in sports, games, and events all fall under this category. Recreation is extremely helpful for using the parts of your brain that you don't habitually engage throughout the day, creating balance. This re-creates your entire physiology and regulates your whole being. It is extremely important, if not essential. Unfortunately, many people do not honor or take the time to enjoy recreation because they are too busy. It rarely is a priority and becomes overlooked despite the fact that recreation can significantly reduce stress.

Recreation Suggestion: Take time to do something you really enjoy that you don't have to do each day. Even if it's only for twenty to thirty minutes, make the time. It will rejuvenate you, refresh your mind-body-spirit, and lower your stress.

Physical Health

Physical health is an aspect of everyone's life that is undeniably essential. What you eat and drink, how you exercise, whether you sleep well, to what extent you attend to your appearance, all of these are part of this area of life. Your doctors, family, friends, fitness instructors, life coaches, and health food store owners, just to name a few, are very willing and able to guide you toward improved health. The media — commercials, advertisements, documentaries, magazine articles, blogs — are forever telling you what to do to feel healthier. Yet stress can seriously affect your ability to follow the helpful advice that is being offered. Why can't you follow the great suggestions being offered to improve your health? You are too stressed! The truth is a calm state of mind will be open and able to follow the myriad of helpful suggestions to honor and improve your physical health in a natural, effortless way.

Physical Health Suggestion: Listen to your body's wisdom. If you have energy, take time to exercise, in a way that's natural for you. If you feel fatigued, then rest. If you feel uncomfortable after eating a certain type of food, remember to beware of that food in the future. You have an inner intelligence that knows how to balance your physical health. Cultivating awareness of this inner intelligence is the key.

Work and Contribution

Many people complain about their jobs and suffer from too many work responsibilities. Many people work because they have to, not because they want to. It seems that work and stress have become synonymous. All work is a contribution, whether you are paid, volunteer, or perform chores around the house. Honoring contribution brings a sense of accomplishment, satisfaction, and inspiration to your day. It also cultivates balance with the larger community. Contribution is gratitude in action. If you see work as contribution you can change your negative perception to a positive one.

Contribution Suggestion: Next time you have resentment or frustration related to a work task, become aware of who will benefit from this action. Shift your perception away from your own negative feelings to the positive result others will enjoy.

Education and Learning

Education refers to all learning, formal as well as informal. It includes the entire gamut of acquiring new information from taking college coursework toward a degree to exploring a word you are unfamiliar with using the Internet. You are hardwired to learn constantly. When you lose your interest in learning due to feeling excessively stressed you negate an important aspect of growth and development. This can result in your balance being seriously compromised. Honoring the innate need to learn is extremely important for mental health and wellness.

Education Suggestion: Every day, look up something you know little to nothing about, listen to a song you never heard, read a poem you never saw, or try a food you never ate. Learn about anything new each day.

Prosperity, Finances, and Possessions

Prosperity is a state of mind. When looking at the important aspects of life, prosperity must be one of these essentials due to the necessity of acquiring certain possessions to assist in a stress-free existence. There is nothing wrong with having financial resources and belongings that enhance life and bring more ease into your day. Honoring prosperity not only includes acquiring more, it also covers the need to downsize and streamline what you already have. Appreciation and awareness of what you have as well as attending to a plan for acquiring what is needed, will lower your stress and cultivate more balance in your life.

Prosperity Suggestion: Practice focusing on what you have instead of what you don't have. The feeling of lack is a stress-producing guarantee. As you become more aware of what you already have, gratitude follows. This leads to a prosperous state of mind and can open opportunities for receiving what you do need.

Prioritizing your Yantra

Now that you have increased awareness of the Eight Essential Areas, you are ready to take the first step to create your own personal yantra. Here's how it works. Look at all eight areas of life and decide which one is in your awareness the most, for good or for bad. The details don't matter, it's about the attention you give it. Sometimes you inadvertently honor the very things that are stress-producing for you because that's where your attention goes. As the law of attraction states, energy flows where attention goes. The area that is in your thoughts and feelings the most, designate as #1. Then number the other seven areas most to least, in reference to energy spent mentally, emotionally, or physically. This is your current baseline.

The second step is to renumber your yantra, but this time designate #1 as the most important area to you if you could have the life of your dreams, with no barriers in the way, no censorship. This is your chance to pretend and fantasize about what you really want without screening anything out as "impossible." This is not a goal-setting activity, it is a values clarifications exercise. When you are done numbering one through eight for your perfect life, use it as an intention tool. Each day, sit in a comfortable chair, relax your body, practice a few minutes of LSF Meditation, and then envision each area starting with your most important one as if it was already happening the way you want it. Feel the feelings you would have if each area was perfect and already in motion. Imagine using all your senses to experience it as if it was already happening. If you cannot envision it in your mind, there is less a chance it will actually happen in reality. Thoughts become things. At the very least, this routine will help your mind think positively, you will feel more uplifted, and you are setting the stage for life to put things in motion to actually make progress toward your intention.

Warning: Beware of "should-ing". Do not choose what is important by what other people tell you is important, or the norms of society. Be genuine, authentic, and bold in your choices. This is just for you, nobody else. It is a guilt-free exercise! It is a wonderful way to honor your needs and love yourself. To love and honor yourself you have to acknowledge all sides of yourself, even the ones you have trouble with. This is the secret to true balance: inner inclusiveness. Also, remember your priorities often change with life circumstances and personal evolution. Feel free to change how you designated the yantra sections as your priorities shift. Finally, envision using positive affirmations, not negative wording: For example, "I want to have less anxiety" can be reworded to say "I want to feel calm." "I want to lose weight" can be reworded to "my stomach is flat and I weigh 140 pounds."

Review the suggestions for each of the Eight Essential Areas daily, and practice the envisioning exercise whenever possible, but at least once per day. By honoring all areas of life, your overall balance will improve, and a sense of well-being and fulfillment will naturally become apparent in your life.

LSF Takeaway #18

Too much physical, mental, and emotional attention on only certain areas of life will inevitably cause an increase in stress. By being aware of the eight universal aspects of life, honoring each of them regularly, you will improve balance and lower your stress.

Since honoring all Eight Essential Areas brings awareness and balance into your life, imagine having one day to practice all eight? If you are able to take a day off to try this idea, here is a sample schedule to follow as a general guideline, changing the order of the itinerary as needed. If you cannot take a day to honor all eight areas, increase awareness of how often you pay attention to each area every week. If you notice you are ignoring certain aspects of your life, have the intention of putting more focus on that area the following week. Notice how your overall feeling of fulfillment and happiness increases with this practice.

Daily Schedule using the Eight Essential Areas

Morning Ritual: Physical Health, Mental Health, Spirituality

- 15 minutes: Get up, use the bathroom, brush teeth, freshen up, drink a tall glass of water
- 30 minutes: Meditation, Prayer
- 60-90 minutes: Exercise

- 45 minutes: Coffee, tea, or morning beverage and light breakfast; inspirational reading
- 60 minutes: Shower, prepare for the day

Mid-Day Activities: Contribution, Education, Prosperity

- 120 minutes: Work and chores around the house: cleaning, vacuuming, dusting, organizing, throwing things out, laundry, etc or outdoor tasks (if applicable)
- 30 minutes: Review your weekly/monthly budget and check for what was spent and what is left; balance checkbook or review your online banking; throw out a few unnecessary items
- 60-90 minutes: Read or explore topics on the Internet you want to learn more about or watch a documentary
- 60-90 minutes: Prepare and enjoy a meal

Evening Wind-Down: Recreation, Relationships

- 60-90 minutes: Do something enjoyable and fun or something creative and inspiring
- 60-90 minutes: Contact friends or family through phone, text, email, messaging, social media or visit them in person
- 30-60 minutes: Before going to sleep, de-activate your mind by listening to relaxing music, taking a bath or jacuzzi, using relaxation apps or YouTube videos, viewing beautiful photos, reading inspirational prose or poetry, journaling, meditating again, etc.

CHAPTER 19

Stress to Success in Six Months or Less

Now that the theories, explanations, and descriptions of how to live stress-free have been presented, it is time for the nuts and bolts practical reality of how to get there as soon as possible. Six months is a fair estimate for how long it will take to successfully change and sustain patterns of thinking and ways of perceiving your life. After reading the previous chapters, your mind and body have already been exposed to new ways of experiencing life with less stress and you may have already started the transformation. This chapter is designed to give you additional guidance and direction to help you progress with ease.

Since these six recommendations help you go from stress to success, I would like to define success from the perspective of Living Stress Free. If you look up the definition of success in the Merriam-Webster dictionary, it states: "the fact of getting or achieving wealth, respect, or fame." The Oxford dictionary defines success as: "the accomplishment of an aim or purpose." Wealth, fame, respect, and accomplishment may be what some people deem as the goal, but I'd like to suggest it's more than that. Success is fulfillment. This fulfillment is achievable in all areas of life. What good are wealth and fame if you have bad relationships or your health is precarious? Feeling fulfilled means that stress is not interfering with your life; stress is not bothering you. You are honoring all areas of your life and have a sense of inner joy and contentment. You love all parts of your life. This is true success!

The next six suggestions are meant to be used as follows: one suggestion per month for the next six months. The suggestions are more than just a specific practice to do each day or a task-driven homework assignment. These recommendations are particular mindsets that you can incorporate into the activities of your day. All that is required is to remember the suggestion each day, preferably when you wake up, and then a few times throughout the day. You can even put a few sticky notes around your house or office to remind you. What works for me is to keep an insight journal. Whenever I'm working on developing a new way of perceiving life, I write down my insights when I notice myself seeing things differently, behaving in a new way, or having new feelings or thinking patterns. It is very helpful to see it written down because it reinforces the changes. I highly recommend keeping an insight journal for yourself, especially when applying the following recommendations.

Suggestion One: Stop Rushing

Rushing takes you out of the present moment and thrusts you into the future. Since rushing is usually due to worry, it cultivates anxiety. The worry about being late, missing a meeting or class, not having enough time to get everything done, the reasons for rushing go on and on. Worse yet, you can become so identified with rushing it becomes your natural state. You walk fast, eat fast, talk fast, drive fast, do chores quickly, perform actions so rapidly that you no longer are aware of the action, only the goal of getting it done. One day, when you cannot rush anymore, and you look back on life, it will feel like something is missing. Something was missing! The present moment was missed because of the constant focus on the future.

This month, intentionally slow yourself down. Each morning, remind yourself to slow down. While you sip your coffee, take your time; taste the coffee fully. Drive a little slower to work; notice the sky, trees, and other scenery as you drive. Walk a slightly slower speed; feel your body walking. Talk a little bit slower; listen to your voice. Plan to get up slightly earlier if you need more time. Don't try to get through the day —experience the day.

With this mindset, life will feel more fulfilling and you will complete your actions with more ease and attention. You will enjoy the moment you are in instead of trying to get out of it for the next moment. This is mindfulness in action. Write in your journal at the end of each day your insights into what it felt like to slow down. Notice how your perception of your day can be a whole new experience.

Suggestion Two: Ego-Busting

Things happen "~~TO ME~~." Ego-busting takes the "you" out of the situation. Many times when you get angry or upset, it is because of personalizing the situation. Have you asked yourself: "Why does this always happen to me?" " See, this is just how I am, I can't seem to get anything right" or "It figures, good things never happen to me." This way of perceiving life is a fast track to creating stress every time. Worse yet, it often becomes habitual. The more you personalize issues, the more likely you will do this automatically, and experience chronic disappointment and frustration.

The truth is, things don't happen to *you*, they just happen. Does a tornado decide which house to destroy ahead of time? Did the stock market drop to compromise your bank account on purpose? Did your favorite sports team lose just to irritate you? These things just happened and it was not personal.

This month, perceive everything that comes your way in a non-personal way. Have the mindset that whatever happens, it has nothing to do with you. If someone doesn't say hello when you greet them in the morning, don't take it personally. Maybe the person is preoccupied with an issue. If you aren't invited to a friend's wedding, instead of assuming they purposely didn't want you to be at this event, try entertaining the idea that they had limited space for whom they could invite. If you get a headache, instead of thinking,"I have a headache," just label it as "headache." Take the "I" out of it. The less you personalize anything, the less your ego will interfere with your life and the easier it will be to calmly go with the flow. Write in your journal each day what it felt like to adopt the "things happen" perspective.

Suggestion Three: More Body, Less Mind

Most people are in their head significantly more than they are in their body. As a society, it seems we are addicted to thinking. Social media has magnified this tendency giving anyone an open forum to share their thoughts and feelings on any subject at any time. People hold onto their ideas and beliefs so tightly they often block their ability to notice anything else. Some people are afraid not to think so they concentrate on their thoughts all the time. Other people feel in control of this unpredictable world by incessantly strategizing, planning, and scheming the best direction to go in life as often as they possibly can. This way of living can be detrimental if there is any interest in lowering stress, feeling relaxed or increasing overall awareness to cultivate a satisfying life.

Try the 60/40 rule: Feel your physical body throughout the day. Feel your energy level, your muscles, your movements, your breath. Feel yourself interacting with the physical space around you. Remember what it feels like to walk through water in a pool, lake, or ocean? Have that same awareness as you move through your daily tasks. Be especially aware of the exhalation of your breath as you perform your actions throughout the day. Have the intention of feeling your body and breath 60% of the time and reduce your attention on your thoughts to 40% of the time. Write your insights and experiences of this in your journal.

Suggestion Four: Stop Judging

Any sense of separation, such as "us and them" thinking, cultivates fear. If there is the familiar on one side and the unfamiliar on the other, anxiety naturally increases. Feeling connected and equal to those around you will increase feelings of security, calmness, and even love. Have you ever been to a professional sporting event? When you sit with the crowd of people all cheering for the same team it feels comfortable, joyful, and secure. It's easy to make friends quickly with those around you and it feels good.

In the same way, when your thinking mind is embracing the commonality and connectedness between people and things, it feels content. When the thinking mind finds fault, criticizes, judges or decides what should or shouldn't happen, it feels discontent. Discontent = Stress. If you are serious about reducing stress in your life, the judgmental mind needs to be tamed. This fault-finding tendency occurs both toward others as well as toward ourselves. If a new habit is formed of acceptance, embracing what is, and allowing both ourselves and others to be genuinely who they are without criticism, the mind will feel more at ease and loving feelings will increase.

For the next thirty days, make a pact with yourself to refrain from judging yourself or others. This means drop the word "should" from your vocabulary. Let go of designating people or yourself as good or bad. Allow and accept. If this feels wrong, recognize that opinion is also a judgment. Use your journal to write down your experiences of this practice. A non-judgmental mindset cultivates ease, calmness, and loving feelings towards yourself and others. It will definitely decrease and prevent stress.

Suggestion Five: Tolerating Discomfort

If I had to identify the single most important skill that every person would benefit from developing, it would be tolerating discomfort. I have come to this conclusion by providing therapy and counseling to a wide variety of clients from different generations, educational backgrounds, cultures, economic categories, etc. This is also a realization from my own practice of meditation and yoga. If someone has not learned how to tolerate discomfort they will not thrive in this world.

Discomfort always has existed and always will. The moment we were born we had discomfort. According to the essence of the Four Noble Truths of Buddhism, all existence is suffering. Discomfort and suffering are one and the same. The idea of original sin in the Christian tradition can be interpreted as original discomfort. Sin feels uncomfortable. Life as we know it was never intended to be Shangri-La.

If you are reading this book, you most likely experience stress on a regular basis and have learned to tolerate discomfort enough to function relatively well. You probably learned ways to distract yourself when feeling bad, practiced forcing positive thoughts into your mind, or numbing your feelings through a myriad of products and substances available to help you feel less mental or physical discomfort. You may be similar to many people I know who do too much for others, constantly trying to help them feel less discomfort, as an avoidance of feeling their own discomfort. The busier you are, the less you feel.

I would like to challenge you, for one month, to try a different strategy that will feel counterintuitive. Let yourself experience your discomfort. Perceive discomfort as stress. See it as an actual entity that is visiting with you for a while. It needs to be acknowledged and experienced for it to dissipate. If you ignore it, try to push it away, or overindulge it, it will stay. The practice is to honor its presence by allowing discomfort to exist and to feel it fully. Then continue with your day. I am not suggesting you do this practice no matter what, even if you have intense pain or in a crisis situation. Use your common sense and follow medical advice when necessary.

This practice will be challenging. If you are used to suppressing your anger, holding back tears when sad, staying busy to not feel, this suggestion will not feel good. However, learning how to live your life whether you are happy, sad, angry or fearful, whether you have pain or pleasure, fortune or misfortune, with the same equanimity, is success. It is wisdom in motion. Write your insights in your journal.

Suggestion Six: Just Do the Next Thing

Being overwhelmed is a universal experience at one time or another in every person's life. Whether it arises from too much to do or it comes from feeling so stressed, emotionally drained, or mentally fatigued that one cannot move forward, the effect is the same: indecisive, confused, and stuck. When this occurs, it is very difficult to function at that moment. It cultivates frustration, fear, and worry.

One of the main reasons the overwhelmed state develops is due to getting lost in the storyline of your life. Something comes into your awareness, you start thinking about it, those thoughts lead to a commentary or narrative about the situation, and before you know it you've created an entire storyline that has not even happened. It only happened in your mind. This tendency to interact with thoughts and ideas instead of reality is the main reason the overwhelmed feelings start. If you focus on what has to be done next and not engage the mind by thinking about all the things that have to be done, and how you're ever going to do them, you will save yourself a lot of stress.

Moment to moment, task to task living is the suggestion for this month. Like a jazz musician contributing to a song by adding his or her particular riffs to complete a musical performance, stay in the moment and complete your task with the supports that already exist around you. All that matters is the next thing that must be done. The present moment is all there is. The future has not arrived yet and the past is over. Just do the next thing. Remind yourself each day to just do the next thing. When you are overwhelmed, do the next thing. Use your journal to record your experience of this process.

LSF Takeaway #19

Living stress-free is succeeding with ease, and success is fulfillment in all areas of life. Feeling fulfilled means that whatever stressful circumstances arise, they do not interfere with your experience of life after the event passes. The one common denominator to fulfillment that is part of the six suggestions outlined in this chapter is mindfulness. Living in the present moment and perceiving your thoughts and feelings as a transient phenomenon leads to not only a decrease in stress reactions, it prevents stress from even occurring. The most effective way to live mindfully is to establish a daily sitting meditation practice. If you sit in nondirective awareness, you will naturally slow down and notice the moment, de-emphasize your ego, notice your body more, disregard judgmental thoughts by letting them pass, tolerate discomfort, and systematically notice the next thing breath by breath. Stress to success in six months or less can be accomplished just through daily sitting meditation practice as described in Chapter Sixteen. However, including these six monthly suggestions in addition to daily meditation will seal the deal!

CHAPTER 20

Putting It All Together

Once upon a time, we were balanced. We lived in a balanced way. We dwelled in the present moment and our awareness was constant. We had a natural curiosity about our experiences and we allowed all feelings to express themselves spontaneously. It was easy to feel love, natural to have contentment, and effortless to experience joy. Feelings of dissatisfaction arose but passed quickly. This is how most of us were born into the world. It is our default state. It did not go away; we just have to rediscover it.

Stress disrupted our balance. Stress disrupted our balance over and over, again and again. After a while, this stress became our new default state. Since we desire what our current state of mind reflects, we inadvertently have held onto this stressful state through the choices we make, with thought, feeling, and action. It's not that we make bad decisions, we are following the vibrational frequency of our inner state.

Have you ever asked yourself, "Why do I have so much trouble doing the very things that will help me feel better?" This is because like attracts like; stress attracts that which is stressful in its nature whether it's immediate or delayed. For example, the other day I was driving to work, and I made a conscious decision to not put my seatbelt on. I always wear my seatbelt. I contemplated why I didn't want to wear my seatbelt. I had not slept well the night before and I felt somewhat agitated and off balance. Because I felt stressed, I purposely wanted to express that stress by doing something I'm not supposed to do. It's the "I don't care" attitude. At that moment I felt like

I was taking control as if that was supposed to make my stress feel appeased. The reality is, I stayed stressed. If misfortune fell upon me and I got in a car accident, the stress would have been much greater due to the fact I was not wearing the seatbelt. This is how stress creates more stress.

Manage the stress, not the situation. This is the foundational philosophy of Living Stress Free. Since stress seeks out more stress, it is not wise to problem solve anything important using a stressed state of mind. The best strategy is to decrease the stress and then move forward with taking action. Since thinking leads to experiencing feelings which leads to initiating behaviors, it is wise to make sure thoughts and feelings are in a balanced state to engage in the best course of action.

Throughout the chapters in this book, you have been given many strategies to decrease and prevent stress. The ability to change your relationship with stressful events by understanding the mechanics of your mind has been described, with many suggestions on how to practice this skill. In this last chapter, I will discuss the final concept to help you on your journey to living stress-free.

> *Before a man studies Zen,*
> *to him mountains are mountains and waters are waters;*
> *after he gets an insight into the truth of Zen through*
> *the instruction of a good master, mountains to him*
> *are not mountains and waters are not waters;*
> *but after this when he really attains to the abode of rest,*
> *mountains are once more mountains*
> *and waters are waters.*
> — D.T.SUZUKI, BASED ON SEIGEN ISHIN

This is a wonderful quote because it explains the process of understanding perception. You perceive something a certain way, you learn a new way of looking at it, and then you go back to the original subject with a new understanding. To clarify, look at "Zen" as your awareness, and the term "abode of rest" as meditation. It reminds me of my favorite T.S.Eliot quote: "We shall not cease from exploration. And the end of all our exploring will be to arrive where we started and know the place for the first time."

You most likely started this living stress-free quest with a stressed mind. You have learned many ways to examine this mind, noticed how it affects you, and increased awareness of all the nuances and tendencies it has. Now it is time to "arrive where we started and know the place for the first time."

Here are three key points you are now ready to imbibe.

1. You do not have to pay attention to every thought or feeling you have. Everything the mind is producing is based on the past. Mind is memory. If you take the concepts in this book to heart and practice living in the present, why listen to your mind? Whatever your mind is giving you through thought or feeling is not that important. It is entertainment at its best and the seeds of suffering at its worst. You are officially being given permission to not listen to all the thoughts in your head and not get carried away with your feelings. It's just a thought; it's just a feeling. All of this is transitory.

2. Now that you've honored yourself through the concepts and take-aways in this book, stop paying so much attention to yourself. The danger with self-improvement and personal growth is it can cultivate a "me-centered" existence. Balance in all things, right? If you work on yourself too much you cannot exist well with others. The natural homeostasis of living with others will be disrupted. This tendency also breeds self-consciousness, which leads to being uncomfortable in your own skin. A highly regarded meditation master used to teach the following suggestion based on the Advaita Vedanta: "Be the Seer, not the Seen." There is great wisdom in this. Basically, perceive life through your awareness looking out not through the awareness of others looking at you. This only activates the ego, which is the "you" being perceived.

3. Downplay everything. Ever notice how highly successful people don't seem to "sweat the small stuff?" It may be that their success

is partly due to this habit. Reactivity causes suffering. In my work as a therapist, I have suggested to clients, on a very regular basis, to de-emphasize their feelings. Normalizing reactions helps tame the ego. The ego wants to make a big thing about everything: the bigger the ego, the bigger the reaction. If you minimize your reaction, normalize your situation, remind yourself it's not that big a deal, guess what? You will respond instead of reacting. You will flow with reality instead of struggling with your ideas about reality. The truth is, most situations are really not that big a deal, and the ones that are will be quite obvious to all.

You have been placed in the life that is yours right now. There is no escaping it. Whatever happened to bring you to this place happened for a reason. On a certain level you chose it and on another level, it was supposed to happen. Why it is supposed to happen may not be clear right now but it often becomes apparent in time. By resisting your life or having an aversion to your circumstances, you will never be stress-free. Being stress-free is your birthright. Isn't it time you reclaim it?

The Living Stress Free Lifestyle

Embrace circumstances exactly how they are. The art of *allowing* is a powerful tool you can use to transform your relationship with your life. Acceptance is needed, but not to the point of complacency. Trust yourself. Balance the eight areas of your life and move forward with your intentions. Allow what is to be but also remain centered, grounded, and in control of your future. How you live in this moment sets the stage for the future. This is how we control our destiny. Live in this moment with complete awareness and presence. This is living stress-free.

One of my favorite visionaries was Steve Jobs. As the keynote speaker at a commencement ceremony, Steve stated the following to the eager graduates about to launch their brand new lives:

*Your time is limited, so don't waste
it living someone else's life.
Don't be trapped by dogma - which is living with the
results of other people's thinking. Don't let the noise of
others' opinions drown out your own inner voice.
And most important, have the courage
to follow your heart and intuition.
They somehow already know what
you truly want to become.
Everything else is secondary.*

LSF Takeaway #20

- Don't pay so much attention to your thoughts and feelings.
- Be the seer not the seen.
- Downplay your reactions.
- Practice the art of allowing.
- Live in this moment with complete awareness and presence.

I wish you all the best as you embark on this living stress-free journey. If you practice the techniques delineated in this book, you will be able to answer the popular question asked by many: "Can you really live stress-free?" The answer is yes.

APPENDIX
TWENTY-SIX ADDITIONAL LIVING STRESS FREE PRACTICES

Use one suggestion each week to make your life less stressful.
You can also randomly choose one suggestion to practice on any given day.
It is up to you.
In six months you will be well on your way to living stress-free.
The practices are not in any particular order.
You may want to write your insights in your journal when practicing each
suggestion.
Enjoy!

1. Each day this week take time for at least one new "task of inspiration." Examples: read a new poem, listen to a YouTube music video you never heard before, cook a new recipe, try a new machine at the gym, take a different route home from work, etc. Change it up and add a new experience to your day, each day, for a solid week, to cultivate inspiration. This will encourage the creation of new neuropathways in the brain to holistically improve your experience of fulfillment in life.

2. Practice one week of no expectations. Whenever you catch yourself desiring a particular result related to a person's actions, how a project will be completed, what the weather is going to do, or finishing your to-do list, just to name a few examples, release the expectation, drop the assumption, and sit with the uncertainty. Becoming comfortable with not-knowing is an essential practice for living stress-free, and is the secret weapon for experiencing happiness and ease in your life.

3. Have the mindset of complete impermanence for one week. Every task you engage in, from the simplest to the most involved, pretend it is the last time you will ever do that particular task at that particular time. For example, as you walk from one end of your living space to another, be aware this is the last time you will ever experience

that walk, at that time, in that moment. Having this awareness will transform each moment into a sacred action. The truth is, this is ultimate reality and will bring a freshness into your life that cannot be put into words.

4. Do not question yourself at all for one entire week. No second-guessing allowed. Whatever you decide to do all week, trust that this is exactly what you are supposed to do without question. This will help break the pattern of self-criticizing and self-doubt that leads to increased anxiety and stress. One caution: do not practice this suggestion when you are experiencing too much stress or you are in a crisis state. The stress will affect your judgment and may lead to unfavorable results.

5. Downplay your emotions. Every time you find yourself exaggerating a thought or feeling, minimize the reaction, normalize the situation, try to "take it down a notch." Embrace the attitude "it's not that big a deal." This will help you respond to circumstances instead of reacting. You will be able to let things go with greater ease and de-emphasize your ego's control over your perceptions.

6. Be aware of the air. Wherever you go, whatever you are doing, tune into the fact that the air around you is vast, ever-present, within and without. The air that exists in the room you are in is also in the entire building, the neighborhood, the town, the county, the state, the country, the world. This is a wonderful contemplation that navigates the mind to something greater than itself and causes the ego to become disempowered. Less ego means less stress.

7. Stop asking "why." For one week, let go of the need to know why anything happened and just go with the flow. Although knowing the reason for situations, events and emotions can ease the mind, there often is not an answer to the question. Seeking an answer can cause undue stress and difficulty staying fully present with what is.

8. Practice finding the positive in every negative. There are always at least two sides to every perception. Becoming polarized on one side only leads to much stress in life. It is a helpful practice to intentionally

find a positive aspect to every negative thought or feeling. Taking the time to find the helpful side of all things is a powerful spiritual practice and can ease mental distress.

9. Prioritize sleep for one week. Go to bed earlier or get up later. Make sleeping more important than all the other tasks you have to accomplish. If you have a rigid routine that requires you to sleep less and do more, purposely take a break from this for one week. This will help balance and honor your body and mind, increasing effectiveness when you go back to your routine.

10. See your mind as a sense each day. Remind yourself that your mind is creating thoughts automatically like a machine performing its function. Just as your eyes see things, your ears hear things, your nose smells things, your tongue tastes things, and you feel things that you touch, your mind is a sense performing its duty. This awareness will help you remember you are not your mind; you are not your thoughts; you are not your feelings.

11. Take a picture each day of something that catches your attention in some significant way. Mindful photography is a wonderful practice to get out of your head and expand awareness of your environment. The picture is just for you. The only purpose is to remind you of a moment from your day. This adds a layer of appreciation to your experience of each day leading to more fulfillment and awareness of presence.

12. For one week do not resist anything. If you are asked to do something at work, just do it without resentment. If your spouse or friend wants to go somewhere, just go without hesitation. If a therapist or physician suggests you do something to improve your health, follow it. This lack of resisting anything is a form of surrender. Surrender annihilates the ego. Remember ego = stress. The only caution to this practice is to have discrimination. If someone who is an unhealthy, toxic person asks you to do something negative, use your common sense, healthy judgment, and intuition to make the choice to set the needed limit.

13. Notice the spaces between things. We are very accustomed to paying attention to form over formlessness. In art, they call formlessness the negative space. This week, make a habit of increasing your awareness of the spaces. For example, when you look at a tree, notice the spaces between the branches and not just the branches and leaves. When you look at cars on a road, notice the distance between the cars. This is a wonderful practice that can be done anywhere: spaces between furniture, the sky between the clouds, the dirt between the pebbles and rocks, etc. The expanded awareness that results from seeing the bigger picture can be transforming and leads to more fulfillment in each moment.

14. Notice the silence between sounds. We are accustomed to paying attention to sounds, noise, people talking, birds chirping, the instruments playing in a song, etc. For one week, create a new habit of hearing the silences. Listen to the pauses between the words when someone speaks, listen to the rests in the music, hear the spaces between the melody of a bird's song. The practice of increasing attention to silence is extremely helpful to rest the mind. Just as there are silences in the midst of sounds, there is silence between your thoughts. Awareness of this is essential to living stress-free.

15. Drop the need to feel special, desire acknowledgment, look for compliments or demand credit for your ideas. Practicing this for one week will help set the stage for continuing this habit indefinitely. It is extremely helpful to become free from the need for any kudos. If recognition comes your way, great, but the wishing for it only leads to feeling stressed. The truth is, feeling special is a product of the ego. Only the ego wants to feel special. Anything that supports your ego will support your stress.

16. Practice mindful walking daily for one week. Choose 5-10 minutes each day to walk just to walk. Have no destination, no goal, no purpose but to experience your body walking. This is not walking for exercise or walking to enjoy nature. It is walking to feel what walking feels like. You can do this in your home. The slower you walk,

the more mindful you will be. By practicing mindfulness as you walk, you will begin to practice it naturally when you perform other actions throughout the day. Mindfulness in motion is a wonderful technique to cultivate living stress-free.

17. Practice letting go of hope and fear. Hope and fear reinforce the ego and the thinking mind. Hope is based on ideas and beliefs, projecting your ego's desires onto an unknown future. Fear is also based on an unknown future that your ego decides will not go well. Since nobody can know the future, and the future is filled with all possibilities, it only drains mental energy to entertain any ideas about it. Trust that what will be will be and act accordingly. Any focus on what might or might not happen in the future takes you out of the present.

18. Create a daily meditation ritual each day this week. Whether you have established a meditation practice or not after reading this book, try to "kick it up a notch." Choose what time of day will work best. Meditate in the same place each day for the same amount of time. Make it more special by wearing a meditation outfit that is loose and comfortable, light a candle, burn incense, or add whatever else makes the experience sacred for you. The consistent practice of meditation as a sacred ritual will reinforce the experience as valuable and help you continue it on an ongoing basis.

19. Pretend you are that which you seek. Identify with living stress-free. If you want to feel happy every day, pretend you have already achieved it. Smile, be cheerful to others, say positive statements, compliment others, enjoy your tasks. If you want to feel relaxed and calm, pretend you already are. Walk slower, breathe deeper, go with the flow, perform actions with ease and effortlessness, take breaks, and fill your mind with peaceful images. Sometimes the aphorism "fake it till you make it" is exactly what is needed to shift identification and create the change you need.

20. Practice mindful eating for one week. Take time to really taste the food you are eating. Use all your senses to experience eating. This

will require slowing down, removing distractions, and making the meal a sacred event. Mindfulness masters recommend eating in silence, appreciating each bite of food before taking the next one. How you use your utensils is part of the experience. Allow the whole experience to be slow, smooth, flowing, and special. If you can only manage this for one meal each day, practice it once per day. The result will change your experience of eating and bring you an amazing connection with the present moment.

21. Go beyond praise and blame for one week. Whenever you try to blame yourself or someone for something that happened, or praise yourself or someone else for an event that occurred, let it go. Release the need to qualify situations. The need to place praise and blame on others or yourself breeds duality, polarizes situations, and feeds the ego. Remember ego = stress.

22. Take a mental snapshot of every place you go as if it's the last time you will ever see it. There are so many times we are oblivious to our surroundings due to being lost in thought. If you remind yourself to look around at your environment, see your surroundings and appreciate where you are, you will experience presence: the "is-ness" of now. This will cultivate curiosity and develop more fulfillment in life.

23. Have agenda-free conversations. For one week, every time you have a conversation with someone find out more about them and listen mindfully, attentively, and openly. Many times we consciously or unconsciously have an agenda when we talk to others. We want them to listen to us, validate our feelings, agree with our opinion, support our cause or do a favor for us. All of this is feeding our ego. Make the conversation about the other person. Your relationships improve and you often will be exposed to new ideas and perceptions that can enrich your life.

24. Each day this week do something you have been putting off doing. It might be throwing out old papers, dusting the blinds, vacuuming the car, bathing the dog, organizing your clothes, writing your

friend, etc. Choose an increment of time that's doable. In most cases, the amount of time needed to complete the task is less than your mind tells you. Tasks you put off are usually due to having too much to do and feeling overwhelmed by it all. Feeling overwhelmed distorts perception. Just chip away each day at something. After the week is through you will most likely feel lighter, more confident and stress-free.

25. Things happen ~~to me~~. Having the awareness that things just happened and it wasn't personal, will transform your life. Each day, remind yourself **things happen** and take YOU out of the equation. Your ego will fight you on this but stand your ground. Experiencing things as just happening allows for expanded awareness and cultivates wisdom.

26. Make your top priority each day this week to manage your stress, not the situation. Forget problem-solving and put your focus on bringing calmness to your state of mind. Choose inner peace over making a point, arguing an opinion or struggling with an issue. From morning to night, have the intention of lowering your stress level each day, every day.

ABOUT THE AUTHOR

Clinician, music therapist, and mindfulness coach, Marilyn Guadagnino has spent the past thirty years working with different types of people suffering from serious mental health issues. This experience increased her understanding and fine-tuned the best ways to help people of all walks of life relieve their symptoms, suffering, and stress. At the same time, Marilyn embraced her own spiritual journey toward personal development, learning and practicing various yogic and Buddhist techniques to experience existence with an enlivened perspective. In the East-meets-West tradition, these two paths came together much like the melody and harmony of a song, to create a new form of therapy — Living Stress Free®, a branch of the Living Stress Free Program created by Lou Guadagnino.

Marilyn has degrees in Music Therapy and Music Education from Shenandoah University. She has worked for the University of Rochester's Department of Psychiatry since 1991 as a clinician and music therapist. In 2005, she became a NYS Licensed Creative Arts Therapist. An accomplished flutist, Marilyn has performed with local orchestras, chamber music ensembles, and Torchx2, an instrumental duo who recorded a relaxation CD entitled "Songs From the Eye of the Storm."

Marilyn and her husband Lou started their own company in 2011, Living Stress Free Inc, devoted to helping anyone reduce their stress and live a healthier, happier life. Living Stress Free afforded Marilyn and Lou an opportunity to offer classes, workshops, retreats, online courses, and individual services to clients experiencing stress overload. Marilyn created an innovative technique, LSF Nada Meditation, to help people experience mindfulness meditation using music and sound, recording "Quiet Cloud" and "Breath as Mind - Mind as Breath," to instruct listeners on this new technique. She started her private therapy and counseling practice in 2013, combining traditional psychotherapy, life coaching, music-sound therapy, and mindfulness training.

Marilyn is a healer. Healers are creative, unpredictable, and inspired. Healers look for holistic solutions and natural strategies to improve health and well-being. The Living Stress Free Bible, Marilyn's first book, is a comprehensive, inspiring source of wisdom, representing the culmination of Marilyn's insights and experiences, and the foundational techniques that Living Stress Free Inc imbibes.

For more information on how to access Living Stress Free Counseling, please visit www.livingstressfree.org

ABOUT LIVING STRESS FREE INC

In 2011, Marilyn and Lou Guadagnino co-founded Living Stress Free Inc. a company dedicated to helping people reduce and prevent stress, increasing health, happiness, and success through counseling, coaching, classes, workshops, corporate training, and retreats.

The Living Stress Free vision is to help everyone live a more fulfilling life. Fulfillment means honoring all aspects of one's life, in a healthy, balanced way, without judgment. This is the LSF lifestyle. Living Stress Free not only offers specific strategies to lower stress, LSF has an entire system designed to transform lives.

The LSF Meditation technique is extremely unique. Unlike other forms of meditation, our technique requires no concentration and no need to stop the mind from thinking. It is a form of nondirective meditation — effortless mindfulness. The practice is simple, pleasurable and effective.

The Living Stress Free Wellness Program has been sold internationally to people looking to reduce their stress and live a more fulfilled life. Spanning three continents, customers have shared how the techniques and practices taught in this program have transformed their lives.

LSF Nada Meditation is an innovative music-sound technique exclusive to Living Stress Free, providing a unique opportunity to experience the vibrational influence of sound on the mind-body-soul to enhance mindfulness meditation.

Marilyn and Lou Guadagnino have taught the LSF system to hundreds of individuals as well as Corporations and School Systems. They were featured on WXXI Radio in Rochester, NY speaking about mindfulness meditation. LSF published two books: It's Never Too Late To Do Nothing - Mindfulness Meditation, Yoga and Spiritual Intelligence as well as The Living Stress Free Wellness Program.

For further information about Living Stress Free® products and services, or to schedule Marilyn and Lou for a presentation or retreat, eCounseling, eCoaching, or eMeditation, please visit www.livingstressfree.org

Made in the USA
Middletown, DE
19 November 2018